Face the Music
A Guide to Infusing Music in the Elementary Classroom

Jana R. Fallin, Ph.D.

THOMSON

Australia • Canada • Mexico • Singapore • Spain • United Kingdom • United States

THOMSON

Face the Music
Jana R. Fallin

Custom Editor:
Ann Veith

Project Development Editor:
Spring Greer

Marketing Coordinators:
Lindsay Annett and Sara Mercurio

Production/Manufacturing Supervisor:
Donna M. Brown

Project Coordinator:
Jacey Berecek

Pre-Media Services Supervisor:
Dan Plofchan

Rights and Permissions Specialist:
Kalina Ingham Hintz

Senior Prepress Specialist:
Kim Fry

Cover Design:
Krista Pierson

Compositor:
Thomson Learning

Printer:
R. R. Donnelley

© 2006 the Thomson Corporation. Thomson and the Star logo are trademarks used herein under license.

Printed in the
United States of America
1 2 3 4 5 6 7 8 9 08 07 06

For more information, please contact Thomson Custom Solutions, 5191 Natorp Boulevard, Mason, OH 45040.
Or you can visit our Internet site at www.thomsoncustom.com

ALL RIGHTS RESERVED. No part of this work covered by the copyright hereon may be reproduced or used in any form or by any means — graphic, electronic, or mechanical, including photocopying, recording, taping, Web distribution or information storage and retrieval systems — without the written permission of the publisher.

The Adaptable Courseware Program consists of products and additions to existing Thomson products that are produced from

camera-ready copy. Peer review, class testing, and accuracy are primarily the responsibility of the author(s).

For permission to use material from this text or product, contact us by:
Tel (800) 730-2214
Fax (800) 730 2215
www.thomsonrights.com

Face the Music / Jana R. Fallin – First Edition
p. 200
ISBN 10: 0-759-35986-5

Acknowledgements

It is with gratitude that I have had incredibly talented graduate students who have helped me field test and edit *Face the Music*. Dr. Connie Hale used the textbook with her classes at Winthrop University in South Carolina. Christopher White taught classes at Dodge City Community College in Kansas using the book, and Meredith Knapp and Susan Holmberg taught courses at Kansas State University with *Face the Music* as the text. These outstanding teachers and their students have provided invaluable suggestions for editing and making the textbook more usable.

The students in my course, Music for the Elementary Teacher, at K-State have also been part of the editing process for *Face the Music*. With gratitude I thank them all. Thanks to my husband and sons who provide continued support for my professional endeavors.

Table of Contents

Preface		1
Section I		3
Chapter 1.	Getting Started	3
	Helps for Better Teaching	
	Madeline Hunter ideas for planning and presenting a lesson	4
	Brunner's Research	5
	Howard Gardner's Multiple Intelligences	7
	Aesthetic Learning/Elliot Eisner	9
	Modalities of learning….aural, kinesthetic, visual	11
Chapter 2	The Basics	13
	Elements of Music	14
	Teaching Rhythm	15
	Games to Use with Teaching Musical Notes	19
	Teaching Melody	20
	Teaching Harmony	23
	Teaching Form	23
	Clever Ways to Teach Theme and Variation	25
	Teaching Tone Color	25
	Teaching Dynamics	27
	Dynamic Markings	28
Section II	Doing What Musicians Do	29
Chapter 3	Listening	29
	Music is the aural art	30
	Listening for directions	30
	Concert Attendance "Fear" and "Rules"	31
	Sound Walks	32
	Rule of Three	33
	The Moldau	34
	"Twinkle, Twinkle Little Star" –"Ah, Vous dirai-je, ma-men"	35
	L'Histoire du Soldat- "The Devil Went Down to Georgia"	36
	Experiences in Listening using Children's Books	39
	Qualities of Good Art	39
	"Hallelujah Chorus" from *Messiah*	39
	Multiple Versions	40
	Listening through the Historical Periods	41
	Listening Maps	42
Chapter 4	Performing	45
	Singing	46
	Anyone Can Learn	46
	Matching Pitch	46
	Natural Chant of Childhood	46
	Helping the Child Not Yet Matching Pitch	47
	Selecting Songs	48

	Playing	Using Charts	49
		Chants and Nursery Rhymes	51
		Categorizing Sounds	52
		Grids	52
		African Rhythms	53
		Native American Stories	54
	Moving	Drums	55
		Sounds for Movement	56
		Movement Games	57
		Musical Games	59
		Native American Word Games	60
		Weikert Research	61
Chapter 5	Creativity		63
		Process versus Product	64
		Torrence Levels of Creative Thinking	64
		Compositional Formula	66
		Body Sounds for Creativity	68
		New Words to Familiar Songs	68
		Creating Visual Guides to Music	69
Section III	Helps for the Classroom		71
Chapter 6	Using Children's Literature with Music		73
		Relating to reading	73
		Catalysts to Creativity	74
		Sound Compositions	75
		Enhancing Reading	75
		Why Teach This Way?	77
		Listing of Books	81
Chapter 7	Using Music with Science		85
		Creating Science Songs	85
		Creating Sound Compositions	86
		Bubble Games	87
		Sound Waves	89
		Palm Pipes and Music	89
		Body Music	91
		Animals, Science and Music	91
		Carnival of the Animals	92
		Swan Lake, "Flight of the Bumble Bee"	93
		"On the Trail"	94
		Games and Activities about Animals	94
		Weather and Music	95

Chapter 8	Using Music to enhance Math Learning	97
	Reinforcing Math Skills	97
	Predicting	101
	Patterns	101
	Musical Notation	101
	Song about Math Facts	104

Chapter 9	Using Music to Understand Our World	107
	Multicultural Student Populations	108
	Multicultural Awareness through Children's Literature and Music	108
	American Story	
	Patriotic Music	109
	Folk Music	110
	Successful Strategies for Teaching America's Music	110
	The National Anthem	110
	"When Johnny Comes Marching Home," "Yankee Doodle"	111
	"America the Beautiful"	111
	Slave Songs	112
	Jazz	113
	The Blues	113
	Gospel Music	114
	Holiday Music	114
	Music of the Wars	115
	Water, Music and the Study of Civilization	115

Chapter 10	Relating to the Other Arts	117
	How to Relate the Arts	117
	Art---Impressionistic Art with Impressionistic Music page	117
	Architecture --- Anderson Hall at Kansas State University	119
	Movement---Walk to the Bunkhouse --- contrasting the smooth/jagged rhythms	120
	Drama---L'Histoire du Soldat –Charlie Daniel's Devil Went Down to Georgia	120

Chapter 11	This and That	123
	Lagniappe for the Teacher	
	Video Taping for Improvement	123
	Memories of Teaching	124
	Encouraging Participation	125
	Speaking of Keys	

Appendices

Face the Music
A Guide to Infusing Music in the Elementary Classroom

You may be asking, "Why *Face the Music* for the title,?"

"Face the Music" is an old saying, and it is the title of a song composed by Irving Berlin, with lyrics "Let's face the music and dance," from a 1936 movie *Follow the Fleet*. It is also the name of a political blog, a band, an album by the Electric Light Orchestra and the title of a movie. The saying may come from the musical theater, where an actor with stage fright would be told to "face the music," meaning turn toward the orchestra pit; a move that would leave the nervous actor facing the audience. The origin of the phrase may also have military roots, perhaps indicating to soldiers in ranks, turn toward the military band.

The saying "face the music" also denotes turning to face responsibility, not hiding one's eyes from the right thing, as in "I know I should return home and 'face the music.'" The usage can suggest facing the consequences of some action.

My friend Dr. James Underwood, the retired Chairman of the Geology Department at Kansas State University, suggested the title to me. One night my husband David and I were having supper with Jim and his wife Margaret Ann, and I was describing my book project. Jim said, "I have the perfect title for the book: Face the Music!" It seemed to fit because this book is different from most texts used to teach music to elementary education majors. Most are much more devoted to teaching music theory and skills.

My belief is that future elementary school teachers need usable, practical musical strategies to infuse into their curriculum. If a college student already knows how to play the piano, that will serve them well, but trying to get a novice to a proficient level during one semester at this point in their career is not a wise goal. A more realistic goal is to give them strategies to incorporate music into their classrooms that are not heavily dependent on their musical skills. These realistic music lessons will in turn help their students learn more efficiently. This is what *Face the Music* offers.

The idea is to get started using music in the elementary classroom, regardless of the complexity of the activity. By "facing the music" a teacher will be able to observe the richness and depth of learning that results from infusing music into the curriculum.

As a little girl, I learned to "face the music" early on. One of my much beloved playthings was a small record player with little colored plastic records, which I believe was a Disney toy. (If I only still had it I could make some money selling it on Ebay!) My favorite of the little records, the yellow one I think, played "Bippity Boppity Boo" from *Cinderella*. That recording was played over and over and over again, probably driving the rest of the family crazy! What hours of fun I had playing those records and singing and dancing around the room! The music made me happy, listening gave me joy; it made me want to move. As the song was sung repeatedly, I was "facing the music."

Perhaps I had some sort of fascination with record players. Daddy won one of those big old-fashioned record players built into a wooden cabinet with doors that opened in front. The whole thing was perched on tall wooden legs, and it came with a lot of heavy black breakable records. He won it selling tires through his store. The record player sat in the living room of our old house, and probably was off limits to me. My memories include playing the recording of "Glow Little Glow Worm" and something with "Spanish" in the title, again repeatedly, and dancing all around the living room with my pigtails flopping along behind me. The memory is vivid, probably because I was disobeying the rules and getting into the record player when I shouldn't!

Some things don't change much. Children today still love to play and sing music. The piece of equipment has changed from a record player to a CD player or a computer, but the effects remain the same: children love music. Astute teachers will use the natural childhood love of music to their advantage, and let it help them teach.

This picture of a friend's grandson is a precious image of the joy of music in a child's life. It's true—children love music.

World Wide Words is copyright © Michael Quinion, 1996–2005. A British viewpoint about international English.

http://alt-usage-english.org/excerpts/fxfaceth.html   Mark Israel gives "accept unpleasant consequences" and also gives origin perhaps military or nervous performer

FACE the MUSIC

CHAPTER ONE

Getting Started

The recipe for biscuits calls for two cups of flour and three teaspoons of baking powder. The amount of flour is much larger, but the leavening agent – the baking powder-- is critically important. Without baking powder, the biscuits will not rise. They will bake into hard, flat objects that are not tasty for eating. This analogy is applicable to the arts in the elementary classroom. When a teacher uses music and the other arts throughout the curriculum, a leavening or rising occurs. Much as baking powder interacts with other ingredients when stirred, kneaded, cut and baked to make delicious biscuits, blending music with other subjects makes the curriculum more interesting and inviting to children. The arts mix joy into the learning environment, enabling young students to interact with the subject matter in ways that enhance and foster the learning process.

Some teachers hesitate to use music in their instruction. "After all, you have to be talented and skilled for that," or "I'm not musically talented," might be the comments. Perhaps unpleasant experiences have influenced these teachers. Someone in the teacher's past might have said, "Just mouth the words while we sing this song," or teenage peers may have teased them about their singing voice while they were "having fun" belting out top 40 songs with the radio. These hesitant teachers may have had ineffective elementary music teachers who made them hate "music." While as teens they continued to buy records and CDs for personal pleasure, belittling and unsuccessful occurrences may have created an ongoing low sense of musical self worth.

> Remember, if you can turn on a CD or tape player,
> you can include music in your curriculum.

Information in this book will provide elementary teachers with concepts and methods for integrating music into their curriculum and for using music to enliven their teaching. Teachers willing to infuse music into their curriculum will discover it is not only a possibility, but also an imperative. What starts as the rare experience will become the norm as teachers see the tremendous results for their students.

Helps for Better Teaching

Several discoveries in the teaching/learning body of knowledge have affected my teaching positively. These came to be included in my teaching storehouse through years of trial and error in the classroom. The ideas selected to share are to help students when they become teachers avoid the same trials and errors. For those beginning in a teaching career, my desire is to help them achieve success in the elementary classroom.

The Instructional Tools

Using Madeline Hunter's ideas for planning and instruction

> Madeline Hunter (1916 --1994) was a California educator whose ideas helped thousands of teachers improve their teaching skills. As principal of University Elementary School, a laboratory School at UCLA, she saw students significantly raise test scores through the application of her ideas, results later replicated in an inner-city school setting. She later served as Professor in Administration and Teacher Education at UCLA. Hunter produced 17 videotape collections, authored over 300 articles and 12 books including *Teach for Transfer, Mastery Teaching,* and other TIPS publications.

She developed a seven-step template to use with lesson planning and teaching. Her model was designed to increase learning for students. Using these steps is a great help for preparing effective lesson plans.

Anticipatory Set

Do something to get the student's attention focused on the lesson. This setting the stage for learning should take place as students are coming into class or are moving from one activity to another. It could be a question posed to the class. Perhaps hold up a paper sack and ask the student's what they think is inside. It could be a review of something previously taught that will be continued in today's lesson. Use anything to draw their minds toward the lesson. Beginning teachers discover that children, like adults, have much to think about. Just because the teacher stands up and starts a lesson, is no assurance that the children are attending mentally.

State the Objectives

As a beginning teacher, I thought telling the children what I planned to teach and what they were to learn was "giving away" the lesson. Madeline Hunter teaches us that telling the students what they are going to learn increases the learning. "We are going to be learning about……. " "By the end of today's lesson you will be able to ………"

Teacher Input

This is the point when the teacher gives information to the students which is needed to accomplish the objectives of the lesson. Possibilities might include using the board, a chart, or the overhead. The information perhaps could be given using a video or a map or PowerPoint presentation. Disseminating information to the students is the goal.

Modeling

Showing an example of what is an acceptable product or process helps learning progress. This could be a poem, a rhythmic composition, steps to follow in the group, correct documentation of the group's work, or a skill such as "play the drum like this."

Check for Understanding

The teacher takes time to check the student's comprehension of the material. One strategy is to pose a question, having children show "thumbs up" if they agree or "thumbs down" if they disagree. Giving four possible answers and asking children to indicate with their fingers which answer is correct can achieve this step. "Are they with you" is what you are checking.

Guided Practice

At this stage in the learning, involve the students in the plan. The teacher carefully helps students interact with the lesson material. Madeline Hunter indicates this point in the lesson to be crucial for future success. Guiding students to a point where they can accurately and successfully accomplish the material in the lesson insures they can proceed successfully. The learners should go through all the steps of the task, or at least enough so the teacher can judge their predicted success. Walking around and looking at answers, listening to groups as they work, evaluating written material helps the teacher involve the students.

Independent performance

This is the point where the students are asked to independently proceed with a part of the lesson. They will be using the skills or information learned without help from the teacher. Letting students perform the tasks or sing the song or solve the problem without any help from the teacher is essential for practicing the new skill or process. When first using Hunter's plan, I was amazed at how often I jumped in to help.

One experienced music educator, Mollie Tower, former Supervisor of Music for the Austin, Texas, schools, adds a final step to Hunter's points. She suggests a wrap up of the lesson, reviewing what has been learned. To "hammer down" the information presented in the lesson through a quick review brings a completion to the lesson, and helps students process the material as they reflect on the material. It gives students a sense of accomplishment, and will provide a final assessment of the material before moving into other activities.

Applying Bruner's Research

> Jerome Bruner (b. October 1, 1915 in New York) is one of the premier psychologists, philosophers and educational researchers of modern times. Bruner's work has been influential in many areas including moving psychology from behavioralism to cognitivism and eventually to constructivist models, and leading in the creation of the "Head Start" early childhood system. His major works are *The Process of Education* (1960) and *Acts of Meaning* (1991).

Jerome Bruner stated, "we begin with the hypothesis that any subject can be taught effectively in some intellectually honest form to any child at any stage of development." This led to his work in the development of the spiral curriculum, where a concept is introduced at one level and revisited at successive levels and ages, each time with deeper understanding and mastery. The emphasis being that later teaching builds upon earlier experiences to create an even more mature and explicit understanding of the concept.

Another key to Bruner's theories is his emphasis upon the concept of intuitive thinking as opposed to analytical thinking. Where analytic thinking arrives at answers through deductive reasoning using step-by-step processes of scientific inquiry, intuitive reasoning allows the learner to explore a question discovery, instinct and personal experience without the need for constrictive process. The student is capable of a degree of familiarity without the initial inclusion of overwhelming vocabulary, facts and details. Bruner states, "…it may be of the first importance to establish an intuitive understanding of materials before we expose our students to more traditional and formal methods of deduction and proof."

Bruner highlights three key ways in which children transform experience into knowledge: through action (enactive), through imagery (iconic) and through written forms (symbolic). Much of a child's learning involves the negotiation and conflict of these three areas.

> **Enactive** learning --- The child learns by doing. Hands-on activities lead the student to intuitive understanding of any concept. The learner is actively involved in the learning process through manipulatives and participation. For example, a child would sing the notes "me, re, do" on a neutral "loo" syllable, while moving his or her hands in a downward direction, following the movement of their voice.
>
> **Iconic** learning --- Students learn to transform pictures and graphs into representative concepts. A visual icon or illustration provides imagery and metaphor for learning a concept. For singing "me, re, do," the following lines drawn on the board or overhead helps children learn the concept of high and low, and equate singing up and down with perhaps walking up and down stairs.
>
> ―
>
> ―
>
> ―
>
> **Symbolic** learning --- Students are able to transform appropriate symbols, such a notes, into meaning and action. Musically this involves the use of proper notation systems. Further, the student is able to function on an abstract level and draw conclusions regarding meaning and value from the works studied and performed..

For example, show "me re do" on the staff with notes as the last segment of the learning activity.

The implications for Bruner's theories are first to let the student explore and discover concepts through their own meaning-making processes. Learning involves mastering each of the increasingly complex modes, enactive to iconic to symbolic. After allowing the child to make their own intuitive connections, the teacher can guide the student to deeper understanding, using strategies that require analysis, specific terminology and further guided activities as suggested by the spiral curriculum.

Music is unfortunately often taught in the reverse. Students are presented the actual symbolism first. The staff and note names and rhythmic values and all sorts of information are presented and "drilled" in class before any music making occurs. Perhaps this reversal in the learning process is partly the reason many people think they are not musical.

A Different View of Intelligence

> Howard Gardner (b. 1943 in Scranton, Pennsylvania) has been Professor of Education at Harvard since 1986. A student of Jerome Bruner, Gardner assumed co-leadership of Harvard Project Zero from Nelson Goodman in 1971, which as become one of the leading educational research centers in the United States. His *Frames of Mind: The Theory of Multiple Intelligences* (1983) is considered pivotal in modern psychological theory.

Until Gardner's work, 'Reading, Writing and 'Rithmatic' has been more than a line in an old song. Most schools' testing of students has been heavily weighted for reading comprehension and mathematical computation. This is particularly true of standardized tests such as the SAT or ACT or PRAXIS. Since the passing of *No Child Left Behind* educational reforms, American education has seen an even greater emphasis upon assessment in math and reading. Society has long looked at the concept of "intelligent" as only involving areas of deductive reasoning or linear thought. Through his writings and research Gardner has caused a re-evaluation of the way intelligence is viewed, from a single capacity to a set of intelligences that all people possess in varying degrees.

In his *Theory of Multiple Intelligences,* Gardner developed a set of criteria, or signs, to define intelligence based upon analyzing the abilities that enable human beings "to resolve genuine problems or difficulties that he or she encounters and, when appropriate, to create an effective product --- and must also entail the potential for finding or creating problems --- thereby laying the groundwork for the acquisition of new knowledge." His criteria are:

- Potential isolation by brain damage
- The existence of idiot savants, prodigies, and other exceptional individuals
- An identifiable core operation or set of operations
- A distinctive developmental history, along with a definable set of expert "end-State" performances
- An evolutionary history and evolutionary plausibility
- Support from experimental psychological tasks
- Support from psychometric findings
- Susceptibility to encoding in a symbol system

In his original work, Gardner formulated a list of seven areas of intelligence, which he called Multiple Intelligence (MI), while allowing for the possibility of more. The first two we traditionally equate with IQ. The next three are commonly associated with the arts and the final two are referred to as the personal intelligences. Later in his writings Gardner added an eighth intelligence. All human beings possess varying abilities in all intelligences. Our uniqueness comes from the way they combine within each of us. In the first seven intelligences Gardner sites famous people to exemplify his theory, people who expanded their fields into new areas through their work.

The intelligences are:

Linguistic (word smart): Along with logical-mathematical this is the most common area associated with traditional notions of IQ. This entails the ability to understand the use of words to communicate ideas and complex meaning. Individuals are able to express themselves rhetorically or poetically and usually excel in public speaking and/or writing. Examples: T.S. Elliot and Virginia Woolf

Logical-Mathematical (number smart – linear thinking): In Gardner's words, it entails the ability to detect patterns, reason deductively and think logically. Often involving mathematical operations, this intelligence is most often associated with scientific processes. Example: Albert Einstein

Musical (sound smart): Musical acuity is associated with people who are able to think and communicate in sound. Beyond the recognition of pitches, tones and rhythm, these people are able to hear and create forms and structures within the sounds that create expression and meaning. Examples: Wolfgang Amadeus Mozart and Igor Stravinsky

Bodily-Kinesthetic (physical smart): This intelligence encompasses the potential for using one's body to solve various life challenges and express ideas and feelings through gesture. These people are often able to use tools with great precision and timing. Dancers and athletes excel in this area as they use their minds to control bodily movements. Example: Martha Graham

Spatial (shape or picture smart): Often referred to as visual-spatial, this intelligence involves the ability to perceive, organize and transform space. Individuals are able to recognize and use the patterns of pictures, colors and shapes to express thoughts and feelings. Example: Pablo Picasso

Interpersonal (knowledge of others – people smart): This refers to the ability to understand, perceive and discriminate between the moods, feelings and intentions of others. These people are able to work effectively with people and are often seen as charismatic and empathetic. Example: Mahatma Ghandi

Intrapersonal (knowledge of self – self smart): The capacity to understand oneself, have deep understanding and appreciation for one's own feelings, thoughts and motivationsw. These individuals have a high degree of imagination, originality, confidence and independent will. In Gardner's view they have an effective self-model and are able to use it to regulate their lives. Example: Sigmund Freud

Naturalistic (environmental smart): Persons with abilities in this intelligence are able to recognize, categorizes and draw upon features of nature. They are uniquely aware of their surrounding environments and the effect of themselves and other factors upon it. Gardner does not specifically cite examples but one could look to John James Audubon or Jacques Cousteau in this area.

In teaching, remembering these areas, and offering learning opportunities in each will help bring success to the learners. One topic, one concept, one skill could be approached from multiple, or all, areas to bring about deeper understanding and master. One skilled educator, Dr. Mary Ellen Titus, who uses Gardner's MI theory states, "All children are gifted. You just have to discover where."

The Aesthetic Mode of Knowing

> Elliot Eisner (b. 1933 in Chicago, Illinois) has established himself as one of the foremost leaders of arts education and educational reform. As the Lee Jacks Professor of Art and Education at Stanford University he has published over 300 articles and 15 books. Of most significance to this book's purposes are The Kind of Schools We Need (1998) and The Arts and the Creation of the Mind (2002). Eisner is one of the leading thinkers and writers in the area of Aesthetic Education and proponents of Discipline Based Arts Education (DBAE).

As part of the arts-based inquiry movement, Eisner suggests that each art form has the potential to influence experiences and in doing so alter the way in which we understand our world. He asserts that the written word cannot adequately represent all the ways people understand. Eisner outlines seven modes of know: Aesthetic, Scientific, Interpersonal, Intuitive, Narrative/Paradigmatic, Formal and Spiritual.

In establishing the Aesthetic Mode, Eisner suggests that life is primarily qualitative as opposed to the quantitative, fact and numbers-based way schools approach it. The aesthetic mode is a process that can be used to create works of science as well as art. In both cases the creator and/or audience is seeking a "rightness of life" for the problem at hand. He comments, "Scientists, like artists, formulate new and puzzling questions in order to enjoy the experience of creating answers to them." While inclusion or emphasis of the arts is not necessarily the only way to achieve this goal, infusing the arts into other areas of the curriculum facilitates a clearer path to understanding the world in which we live.

The Aesthetic Mode involves the recognition, organization and manipulation of the various forms in all human activity. Eisner states,
- All things made, whether in art, science, or in practical life, possess form.
- Form is not only an attribute of or condition of things made; it is a process through which things are made.
- The deeper motives for productive activity in both the arts and sciences often emanate from the quality of life the process of creation makes possible.

Infusing the arts into our classroom helps transform the way students think and solve problems. Senses are refined and honed so that the world is experienced in increasingly subtle and complex ways. By promoting and exercising the imagination students are able to see, hear, touch, taste and smell that which is not readily accessible. The arts provide new models for making meaning of the world around them and they give unique access and understanding into the parts of human experience that are expressive and feelingful but defy verbal description. Eisner (2002) summarizes:

(1) Humans are sentient creatures born into a qualitative environment in and through which they live.
(2) The Sensory system is the primary resource through which the qualitative environment is experienced.
(3) As children mature, their ability to experience qualities in the environment becomes increasingly differentiated.
(4) Differentiation enables children to form concepts. Concepts are images formed in one or more sensory modalities that serve as proxies (representatives or substitutes) for a class of associated qualities.
(5) Concepts and the meanings they acquire can be represented in any material or symbolic system that can be used as a proxy for it.
(6) The child's developing ability to differentiate, to form concepts, and to

(7) Which aspects of the environment will be attended to, the purposes for which such attention is used, and the material the child employs to represent it influence the kind of cognitive abilities the child is likely to develop.

(8) The decision to use a particular form of representation influences not only what can be represented, but also what will be experienced.

(9) The arts invite children to pay attention to the environment's expressive features and to the products of their imagination and to craft a material so that it expresses or evokes an emotional or feelingful response to it.

(10) A major aim of arts education is to promote the child's ability to develop his or her mind through the experience that the creation or perception of expressive form makes possible.

For Eisner, approaching subjects from an aesthetic basis, where students are allowed to feel, ponder, reflect and create, leads to greater motivation. People have a basic need to lead a stimulating life. He asserts that knowledge is something that one discovers, not something one makes. Teaching students to recognize and understand the various forms of life that defy language, to break down the various forms of any given object or activity, allows the student to apply personal meaning to that object and retain its essence. Through aesthetic experience we can participate vicariously in situations beyond our reach. Students are motivated to inquire, to ponder, to examine, and to learn.

Incorporating Modalities of Learning

People tend to learn through three basic approaches…by listening (aurally), by reading, seeing or watching (visually), or by doing a motion or touching something involved with the learning activity (kinesthetically). Usually one of these modalities will be predominant or preferred in a learner, though they will have some proficiency in all. Individuals who like to read about something to learn it, or prefer watching someone demonstrate "how to" are probably visual learners. Those who enjoy someone telling them about a subject, or like receiving verbal instructions rather than written ones, or who like to learn by listening to a CDRom program are most likely aural learners. Those who enjoy learning by "doing something" through movement, gesture or the use of manipulatives, are in all likelihood kinesthetic learners. Many people are exceptional in more than one modality.

Successful teachers, when planning a lesson, include activities in all three learning modalities to ensure the highest learning occurs in the classroom. Examples include:

> **Aural** --- Including musical opportunities in a lesson will help learners understand concepts and retain information. They can sing songs that include the information, listen to recordings that set mood or exemplify historical settings or culture, or create musical rhymes to organize the information. Music is the aural art.

Visual --- Using visual representation for each lesson will help learners achieve better understanding of the material presented. Writing on the board, including a picture, graph or map and making pictorial representations will resonate with the visual learner.

Kinesthetic --- Adding gesture or movement to a learning activity will greatly help the kinesthetic learner. Drawing in the air, tracing patterns, including sign language, and using manipulatives all serve to reinforce desired outcomes and add an enjoyable element to the learning.

Words to the Wise

By incorporating these learning theories into planning and instruction, teaching will be better received by the students and learning will be improved. We often teach as we were taught, even if it was not the most effective procedure. Teachers aware of learning theories, and willing to use the findings, break the outmoded patterns of teaching.

The strategies recommended in the following chapters often include the theories and research discussed in this chapter. Teachers in the field can conduct their own research, often labeled *Action Research*, by exploring what works best for instructing their own students. An elementary school teacher could group his or her students randomly and try teaching the same material to each grouping of children, but by using a different approach or method with each group. By evaluating the results, the teacher can decide what seems to produce the best results for the students in his or her own classroom. With so much emphasis in education on assessment, gathering data, and using the information to constantly improve instruction, this plan could be very helpful.

Individual teachers, as well as the authorities quoted in this chapter, are professionals involved in the learning process with students. By examining the methods used to instruct within one's own classroom, a teacher becomes a collaborator of those knowledgeable individuals involved in educational research. Hopefully *Face the Music* will empower teachers to explore the treasures awaiting those who use music and the arts as an integral part of the curriculum. Just like the actor with stage fright who had to "face the music" to be effective, teachers choosing to use these proven strategies will become more effective as well.

Note of thanks---It is with gratitude that I have been given wonderful students throughout by career. One of these gifts is Christopher White, a very talented jazz musician and teacher of music. He has provided invaluable help in writing this chapter. He is always a good sounding board, and he is an excellent writer and knowledgeable scholar and music educator as well. The interesting point about Chris is that he was my student over 20 years ago in Lafayette, Louisiana, and now he is again my doctoral student at Kansas State University. How nice to be given a great gift twice.

Chapter 2

The Basics

> Music --- Sounds and Silence moving through time.
> Sounds organized into patterns.

When baking cornbread, the cook starts with the ingredients---cornmeal, flour, sugar, eggs, milk----the ingredients for making cornbread. With music, we also start with the ingredients; only in music we call these basic "ingredients" elements. The elements in music are those basic parts, rather like raw ingredients for cooking, that when mixed together create different types or styles of music.

When tapping a foot to the music, or "keeping time" with the car radio by tapping fingers on the steering wheel, the person is reacting to the element *rhythm*.

When humming a tune, one is remembering the element *melody*, or *pitch* as it is sometimes labeled. (Pitch is an easier term to use with some modern music that has no singable tune, but does have pitch.)

Friends at a picnic singing "Row, Row, Row your Boat" around the campfire are singing a round, creating *harmony*. Playing two or three bells at the same time we label as harmony. The sound from a string quartet or four-part choir also is harmony. Two or more different tones sounding at the same time creates harmony.

The sound sources, what is making the sound in music, are called *Tone Color*, or *Timbre*. When listening to a piano solo, the Tone Color is piano, or keyboard instrument. When listening to a jazz combo, the Tone Color is usually trumpet, keyboard, string bass, saxophone, clarinet and percussion. A recording of a folk singer accompanying herself on a guitar has the tone color of female voice and guitar.

Form is a very interesting musical element, and often one that is unknown to the casual listener. Music is composed with a structure, or form, providing strength and meaning to what we hear. The form helps our ear enjoy the music, much as the form of a building helps give strength to the structure and beauty to the design. Several forms will be discussed including ABA, AB, ABACA(DA) or rondo, and theme and variation.

The louds and softs (quiet) of music are called *Dynamics*. These variances of loudness give interest and variety to the music. It helps make the music more enjoyable and creates tension and release within the music.

Other *expressive qualities* like tempo or speed of the music and texture, how thick or thin it sounds, are sometimes listed as elements. All of these qualities or aspects of the sounds we know as music combine to create special aural experiences for the listener.

THE ELEMENTS

        RHYTHM   PITCH or MELODY   TONE COLOR or TIMBRE

        HARMONY   DYNAMICS   FORM

Under each of the elements, RHYTHM, MELODY, HARMONY, FORM, TONE COLOR, DYNAMICS, the basics can be further delineated into components of each element.

Many classroom teachers are reluctant to include music in their teaching, as they are intimidated or overwhelmed by the multitude of various terms and concepts involved. All those foreign words and strange symbols, how opera singers sound so different from us, so much music history, and so many different styles—one hardly knows where to begin. In seeking ways to simplify the study of music, we find that the elements really fall into rather simple divisions that can be described by pairs using opposite terms.

    High and Low -- (Pitch and Harmony)
    Fast and Slow – (Tempo)
    Long and Short – (Rhythm)
    Loud and Soft – (Dynamics)
    Same and Different – (Form)

In recalling Bruner's Spiral Curriculum, a teacher can start with these basic designations of music, and then begin to deepen the child's understanding by adding complexity to the learning. Thus, High in music might in successive lessons become "Higher" by including sounds that are closer together, yet still higher or lower. The same delineations apply to each category. Fast spirals into faster, slow into slower music, loud into louder and so forth as the teacher helps students learn more and more about the art of music.

By thinking in these terms, rather than using the complex vocabulary, both the musical novice and the young child can intuitively analyze and discuss music with confidence. Playing games with listening by using two bells, one high in pitch and one low, is a start to musical learning. When the children hear the high sound they stand tall with arms stretched overhead, and when they hear the low pitch they crouch down close to the floor with hands tucked around their knees. The teacher is helping them learn to be aware of sounds and listen more carefully, and the activity is just plain fun at the same time! For all the children know, the teacher is just playing a game with the class. Little do they know, all sorts of learning opportunities are beginning for these fortunate children.

The following activities will help a classroom teacher get started with the exciting prospect of including music instruction in the curriculum. The challenge is to observe the learning that takes place for the children. Using music in the elementary curriculum is just like adding spices to cooking---it makes it better.

An Activity using a Nursery rhyme

Teaching RHYTHM

An activity involving the nursery rhyme "One Two Tie My Shoe" is helpful in learning more about the elements.

> One, two, tie my shoe,
> Three, four, shut the door,
> Five, six, pick up sticks,
> Seven, eight, lay them straight,
> Nine, ten, a big fat hen.

Follow the instructions:

1st Say the nursery rhyme "One Two Tie My Shoe."
Pat your hands on your knees as you say this rhyme. If you are patting rhythmically in a steady repeating pattern, you are performing the Steady Beat. This first step might be the only step done with preschool or kindergarten children. You might also let them take turns tapping the steady beat on a drum as they chant the Nursery Rhyme. The children could make the beat faster or slower, louder or softer, as they practice this step in the lesson.

Steady Beat or Pulse The heartbeat of the music. Where you tap your foot or clap your hands.
- Say the rhyme again, putting a mark on the board or a large chart for every steady beat.

| | | | | | | | |

- Count the number of steady beats on the board. Have the children discover how many beats are in the rhyme. The number is twenty, but don't just tell them. Make the children "figure it out". It's part of the fun of the game.
- At the end of the line of beats, draw a double bar which indicates "the end" in music. ‖

2nd Now say the poem, accenting the following words:
(For older children you may go into this activity the same day, but for younger ones, you may want to do it the next day.)

One, Two, tie my shoe. **Three** four, shut the door,

Five, six, pick up sticks. **Seven**, eight, lay them straight.

Nine, ten, a big fat hen. (You have accented some of the beats.)

Accent: A beat that is accentuated or accented.
Often creates sets of beats, usually in sets of 2, 3, or 4 with children's music.

Go to the line of beats you have drawn, say the rhyme again with the group, and mark which beats are accented.

```
 <                  <
 |   |   |   || |   |   |   ||

 <                  <
 |   |   |   || |   |   |   ||

 <
 |   |   |   | ||
```

3rd Now draw a straight line before each accented beat. These straight lines are called barlines, and you have divided the music, or measured it, into groups of four. These groupings are called measures in music.

Of course, when children are learning music in this manner, they are also exploring mathematical concepts as well. These measures of music are actually sets or groups of beats.

```
|   |   |   ||  |   |   |   |

|   |   |   ||  |   |   |   ||

|   |   |   ||
```

Barline: A line drawn before the accented beat to group the steady beats into sets.
It measures the music.

Measures: These sets of beats created by the bar lines are called measures.
Thus, you have measured the music when you divide the music into measures.

4th Next let your hands "speak the words." The teacher can ask the children, "Did you know that my hands can talk?" Clap the rhythm of the words to "One, Two, Tie My Shoe". You are starting to introduce the children to *rhythm patterns*. Sounds can be longer or shorter.

Above each steady beat on your chart or chalk board, decide with the children if the word above the beat has one sound or two sounds. In elementary music, several shorthand versions are used to indicate this. The two sound patterns are called a division of the beat.

| | ⊓
Ta   tee tee

Du   Du Dee

Quarter Note   Eighth notes

The teacher guides the children into making a decision on the beat, or its division, by having the children pat ONE steady beat on their knees while you, the teacher, claps the word. So, the first beat will have the word "One" clapped. Ask the children if this is a single sound (ta) or two sounds, (tee-tee)? They will decide it is a single sound. Above the notated beat, draw a straight line, or a ta. This represents the stem of a quarter note in musical notation. The tee tee symbols represent the stems of eighth notes.

The chart should now look like this:

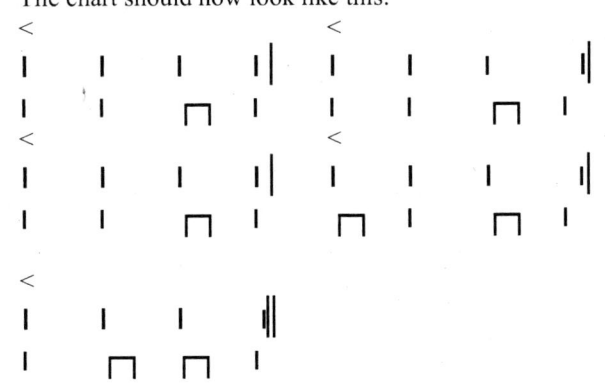

```
  <              <
| |  |  ||  |  |  |  ||
| |  ⊓  |   |  |  ⊓  |
  <              <
| |  |  ||  |  |  |  ||
| |  ⊓  |   ⊓  |  ⊓  |

  <
| |  |  |||
| ⊓  ⊓  |
```

5th At this time, the children can clap the rhythm patterns, play them on percussion instruments, or say different words for the ta and the tee-tee. For example, "Maine" could be substituted for the ta notes and "Kansas" for the tee-tee notes. Or children could say "Coke" for the single sound notes and "Pepsi" for the two sounds of the tee-tee notes. Fast food restaurant names, flower names, car names, candy names, cereal names are only a few categories that will work well. They could select instruments with different pitches, and play the ta words with a higher pitch, and the tee tee words with a lower pitch.

A Word to the Wise: Getting to this point in the activity might take several weeks. The teacher must determine the time spent by assessing student's attention span, their maturity level, and such. For a kindergarten group, six weeks may be needed where a sixth grade group might take only one week.

Introducing Melody

6TH The next step in our nursery rhyme activity is to introduce the element of *melody*. The rhyme can be sung using only two tones, sol and mi. You can use the Kodaly hand signals with this activity. (show drawing of sol and mi hand signs.)
Sing the rhyme using sol and mi and showing the proper hand signs as you sing.

Go back to your chart and decide whether each tone is either a "sol" or a "mi."
Draw two lines as a staff above the chart as shown below.

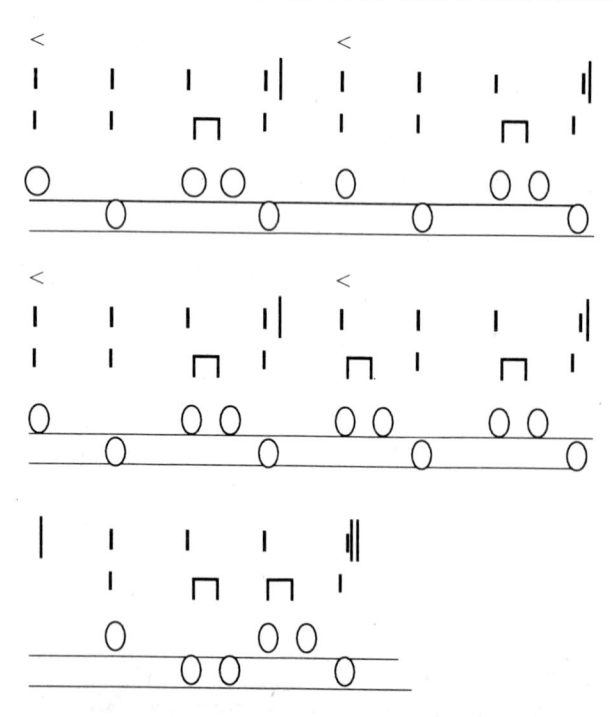

After going through each pitch, the chart should look like this.

Students can perform the melody with the proper rhythm on two keys of the piano, g and e above middle c. Have the student put the right hand pointer finger on g, and the left-hand pointer finger on e. They play as another student points to the music on the board. The sense of accomplishment is incredibly rewarding for these students when they discover they can "read" music and perform it.

An elementary teacher can do this same activity with their own classroom by pacing it according to the interest, ability and attention span of the students. A kindergarten child might only be able to say the rhyme and pat their knees the first day. Then, space the rest of the activity, perhaps over a six-week period. The idea is to introduce the elements in a meaningful way. By sixth grade, students would be able to do much of the activity in one or two days. The entire process can be repeated using another rhyme, verse or poem.

(This rhythm activity is adapted from a process taught by Barbara Grenoble, an outstanding music teacher from Denver, Colorado.)

Games to Use with Teaching Musical Notes

Make a large floor mat by using a heavy clear plastic painter's drip cloth. Using black electriction's tape, make five lines, about 10 inches apart across the wide part of the plastic cloth. These become the lines of the staff. Have children toss a bean bag and name 1st, either line or space, then when children are good at naming lines and spaces, 2nd have them give the names of the line or space (e-g-b-d-f for treble clef lines, f-a-c-e for treble clef spaces), 3rd have them use flash cards with the note on a staff, they name the note and stand on the appropriate line or space. You can do with this game with small groups or in teams and keep score. The staff can also be used for the bass clef. Lines are g-b-d-f-a and spaces are a-c-e-g.

Use staff paper with spaces large enough to hold an M&M, approximately ¼ inch. Give a sheet to each child or each small group. Give a baggie filled with M&M candies. Call out a note name, and the child or group places the candy on the correct line or space. You can also spell using the candies. (Cabbage, Cab, bag, age, are examples of words spelled with names of the notes.)

Use staff paper with spaces large enough to hold a vanilla wafer cookie, approximately 1 inch for spaces. Do the same game, calling out the note name. Children place the cookie on the correct line or space. This gives practice on placing the note ON the line, not above or below, or IN the space. The children can also practice making melody lines, going up or down, or staying the same.

🎲 Use staff paper with spaces large enough to hold the heart-shaped candies popular during Valentine's Day. You can practice note names by placing the candies on the staff.

> With all games involving food, the children can eat them when the game is over. The teacher must be aware of any children with allergies or diabetes, and give them a different treat.

MELODY

In even the most difficult music ever written, the melody can only move up, down, or stay the same.

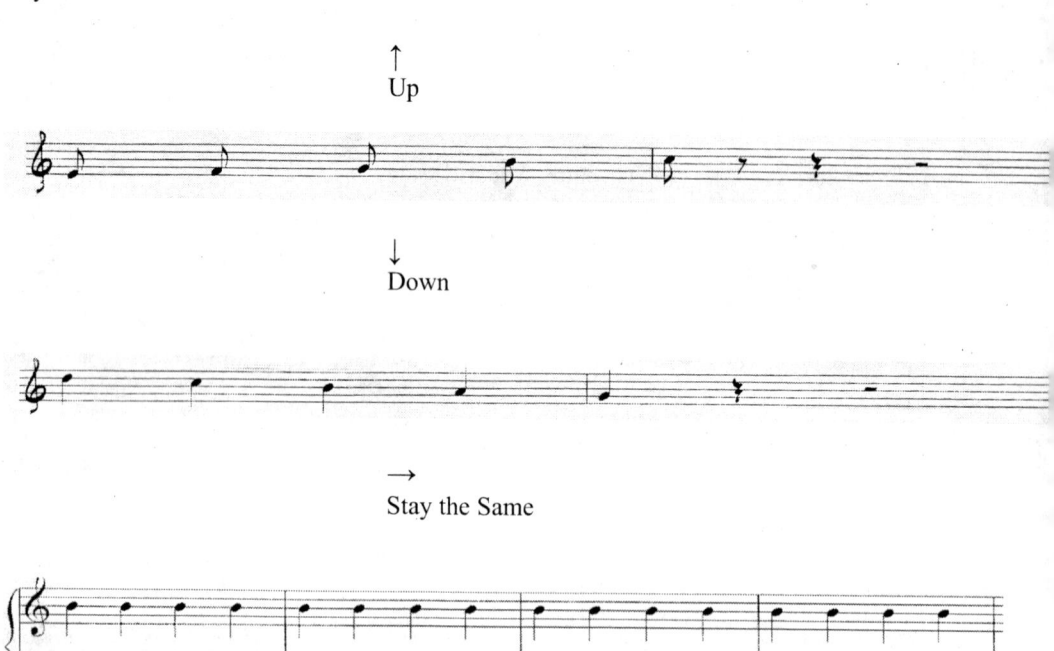

↑
Up

↓
Down

→
Stay the Same

Music moves up and down by step or by skip.

Step:

Skip:

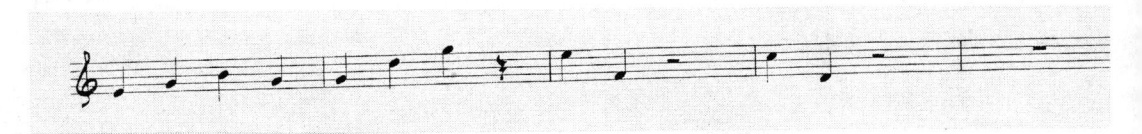

Skips can be large or small.

Large Skip:

Small Skip:

🎲 Use staff paper with spaces large enough to hold a vanilla wafer cookie, approximately 1 inch for spaces. The children can also practice making melody lines, going up or down, or staying the same. They can listen as a child plays a three note melody using bells. Did the melody go up, go down or stay the same? Notate on the staff paper using vanilla wafers. Eating the cookies after is a delicious reward!

The scale is another way melody is organized. These scales help us recognize steps and skips.

Major scales are arranged in a series of whole and half steps. On a keyboard, the half steps are next to each other. Be careful, sometimes a half step is a white key to a black key, but it may be a black key to a white key or a white key to a white key.

Major scales are formed using the following pattern: (— = whole step
½ = half step)

Whole step-whole step-half step-   whole step-whole step-whole step-half step
—   —   ½   —   —   —   ½

The most used scales in children's music are the C, G, F, and D. Music written in one of these scales is said to be in the key of C or G or whatever scale.

    Music in the key of C has no sharps or flats;

    Music in the key of G has one sharp, f#

    Music in the key of F has one flat, b flat

    Music in the key of D has two sharps, f# and c#

C Major Scale:

c   d   e   f   g   a   b   c

G Major Scale:

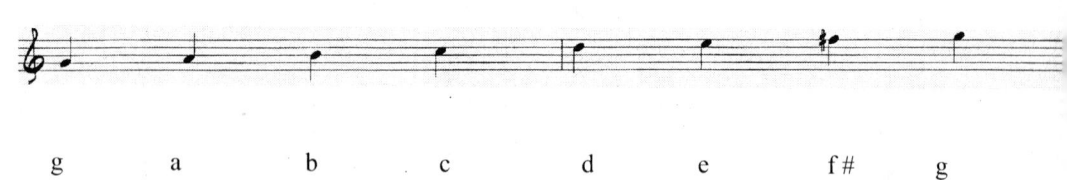

g   a   b   c   d   e   f#   g

F Major Scale:

f   g   a   b-flat   c   d   e   f

Tones arranged in certain patterns can be called a mode. Major and minor are the modes most used in children's music.

A minor scale uses the following pattern of whole and half steps:

Whole step-half step-whole step-whole step- half step-whole step-whole step

    —   ½   —   —   ½   —

HARMONY

Two or more tones sounding together create harmony. One type of harmony is created by chords or triads.

        Chords can be played on the guitar to accompany many children's songs.

        A piano accompaniment to unison singing creates harmony.

        Rounds sung or played create harmony.

FORM

        Music is created with sections that sometimes repeat and sometimes alternate with different sections. These sections create interest for our ears as we listen.
To teach someone to recognize form, first they must be able to recognize "Same" and "Different."

> To assess student understanding of this concept, the teacher can play a game with the children. Have them stand if the tones are different, and stay seated is the tones are the same. Or be pretend robots. For SAME, teachers says, "move your legs like a robot," and for DIFFERENT, "move your arms like a robot." Or, have children hold up a square shape for same, and a circle shape for different.

After learning to hear and see that a melody or phrase is either repeated (Same) or not (Different), students are ready to learn some musical forms.

The sections are often labeled with letter names, and sometimes in children's books, with geometric shapes.

        A   B   A

        ☐   ○   ☐

ABA is a very common form in music. The same section is heard at the beginning and at the end, with a contrasting section in the middle. Children relate to this form as "hamburger form."

        Bun-Meat-Bun

Another example of ABA is an OREO cookie, with the cookie part on each side and the cream filling on the inside. One fun activity is to play an ABA piece (the "March" from the Nutcracker works well) and have the children eat the cookie as they listen to the music, only eating the A part, or cookie on one side, when they hear the "A" section, eating the cream filling when listening to the "B" section, and finishing the last "A" cookie piece when hearing the last A. This activity serves as an evaluation also. By observing them eating the cookie, the teacher can see how well the children understand ABA form.

☐ ○ ☐ ▲ ☐

Another musical form is called a Rondo, where the "A" section is repeated after each differing section. ABACA or ABACADA form is a rondo. This form can be referred to as a "club sandwich" to help children understand rondo form.

        Bread (A),
            bacon, lettuce and tomato filling (B),
                bread (A),
                      egg salad (C),
                            ending with bread (A).

You can let the children design their own club sandwiches to create a sandwich rondo. Select sounds or instruments to represent each part, and play the rondo sandwich.

- A -   Boom whackers could play the rhythm of words "Club Sandwich" for the A section.

- B -   Drums could play the rhythm of "Bacon lettuce tomato" for the B.

- C -   Finger cymbals could play the rhythm of "egg salad, egg salad" for the C section.

Perform this *musical sandwich* with the A B A C A rondo form.

For practice in independent learning, divide the children into small groups, and have each group design a MUSICAL SANDWICH. Perform each composition in class, having the "listening' groups evaluate the success of the "sandwich." Are the sections easily understood? Can others hear the rondo form? *Sam's Sandwich* is a clever children's book to read during this activity.

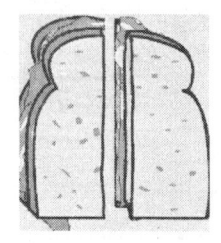

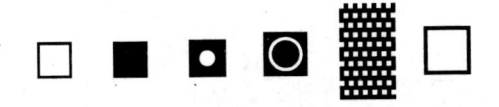

Theme and Variation is another very interesting form to teach children. This form allows the composer to take one theme or melody and change it somehow for each variation. The form is
A   A1   A2   A3   A4   A5   A6, etc.

Clever ways to teach Theme and Variation:
Discuss the potato as theme or A.   What ways can we change the potato? Baked, mashed, au gratin, fried, scalloped, etc. etc.

Use the original Coke can for A, then find all kinds of different Cokes to represent the theme and variation. Use diet Coke for A1, caffeine-free Coke for A2, cherry Coke for A3, diet caffeine-free Coke for A4, etc. etc.

As you play a theme and variation composition (See the Twinkle activity on page   ), display the Coke cans at the appropriate time.

Use potato chips and all those varieties---Plain, Sour Cream, Barbeque, Dill Pickle, Ranch.

Use soups to illustrate different varieties---chicken noodle, tomato, potato, vegetable, or any other example from our world of merchandise and marketing that fits the "variation' model.

Different types of pastas are another way to illustrate Theme and Variation.

TONE COLOR
Tone color is the sound source in music, and is sometimes called *timbre*. An interesting aspect of tone color includes categorizing instruments into groupings labeled as "families." Orchestral instruments are grouped into "families" according to commonalties of the instruments. The four families of instruments are String, Brass, Woodwind, and Percussion. String instruments all have strings. Brass instruments have brass mouthpieces and are made of metal or brass. Woodwind instruments use wind to create the sound, and were once all made of wood. Most have single or double reed mouthpieces. Percussion instruments are struck to create a sound.

String Family Instruments

Violin   Viola
Cello   Harp
Bass

Piano is sometimes included here, but other times included in the percussion family.

Brass Family Instruments
Trumpet   French Horn
Cornet   Baritone
Trombone   Tuba

Woodwind Family Instruments
These are further divided into single and double reed instruments
The mouthpieces of single reed instruments have only one thin piece of bamboo or reed. The double reed mouthpieces have a folded-over piece of very thin reed or bamboo, thus the term double reed.

Flute
(Single Reed)   (Double Reed)
Clarinet   Oboe
Saxophone   Bassoon
                  English Horn

Percussion Family Instruments

Xylophone   Marimba   Tambourine   Maracas
Bass Drum   Timpani or Kettle Drums   Snare Drums
Cymbal   Finger Cymbals   Gong   Triangle
Ethic Percussion Instruments (Cabasa, Agogo bells, Squeeze Drums, Log Drums, Thumb Piano, Bongo drums, etc.)

Several websites have pictures of musical instruments.
> http://www.music-with-ease.com/
> http://classroomclipart.com
> http://cybersleuth-kids.com/sleuth/Art_Music_Cultures/Music/Instruments/index.htm
> http://www.oddmusic.com/
> http://www.usd.edu/smm/
> http://www.freefoto.com

Another method of classifying instruments which is more successful for organizing instruments from all areas of the world includes the labels of *Idiophones, Membranophones, Chordophones, Electrophones* and *Aerophones*.

Idiophones: instruments of material such as metal or wood capable of producing sound by shaking such as a rattle, rubbing as with a glass harmonica, striking as with gongs or bells, or plucking as with a Jew's harp.

Membranophones: mainly drums or instruments that make sound by hitting or tapping a stretched skin.

Chordophones: Stringed instruments that can play several tones simultaneously, as with a zither.

Electrophones: Electronic instruments.

Aerophones: Instruments that require air to be blown in the producing of sound including orchestral instruments such as a trumpet or clarinet and ethic instruments such as a whistle or type of native flute.

With instruments often found in the elementary music classroom, a useful organization plan includes the following classifications:

Shake   Jingle   Rattle   Scrape   Ring

Children can decide on which instrument fits which category by how it is played or how it sounds when played. Drums get their own category. Some teachers designate an area of a cupboard or a set of shelves for storage of the instruments. By lining each shelf with a different colored paper, an easy organizational plan emerges. For example, on the "red" shelf, the shakers could be housed, where as the yellow shelf could be the "jingle" instruments. The colored rolls of paper in the teacher workroom serve well for this system. Around each instrument, teachers or students draw the shape of the instrument using a felt marker. Then, at "clean up time," the children know exactly where to place the instruments.

DYNAMICS
Dynamics are the musical louds and softs included in the performing of music. Using different dynamic levels gives the music variety and keeps the listener interested in the music.

Many musical terms, including dynamic markings, although used worldwide are written in the Italian language. Because the early Catholic Church, headquartered in Vatican City in Rome, had composers writing music and musicians performing music who spoke Italian, the musical terms were written in the common language for communication. These early church musicians also were the ones copying or notating the music for worship services, again most being Italian speakers, so terminology continued to be in Italian. The music would find its way into other countries, and the people would learn to interpret the directions for making music. The Italian terminology was the accepted practice, and continues even today. For example, the early piano was called a *piano forte* because it could play both loud and soft. Through the years, the name was shortened, and we now know the instrument as the piano.

If these early composers and musicians wanted a composition performed quietly or softly, they would write the Italian word "piano" which means soft. For loud, they would use the Italian word "forte" meaning loud. Through the ages, these terms have become, through common usage, employed universally to indicate dynamic markings, tempo markings, and other musical directions. The terms are often designated by only the initial.

Dynamic Markings

ppp	pianissimo	very very soft	f	forte	loud
pp	pianissimo	very soft	ff	fotissimo	very loud
p	piano	soft	fff	fortissimo	very very loud
mp	mezzo piano	moderately soft	mf	mezzo forte	moderately loud

Teaching Tip:

The term "soft" as applied to sound is an abstraction for most children. They are never told to be "soft" by their parents or teacher. They are told to be "quiet." Soft to children denotes feeling or texture; "the teddy bear feels soft." "The towel I dry off with after a bath is soft." Teaching them to associate the term soft with quiet music is no easy step, especially for young children. It is sometimes more successful to use the terms "loud/quiet" to start, and then change "quiet" to "soft" as they begin to understand the concept.

Section II

Doing what musicians do.

Even the finest musician is involved in only three main activities in music.

Listening   **Performing**   **Creating**

In the elementary classroom, the teacher and the students can be musicians, too. They can function as listeners, performers and creators within the boundaries of the class. The following three chapters will guide teachers and their students into activities as listeners, as performers and as creators.

Chapter 3

Listening

Learning to listen,
Learning to hear,
Being aware of the sounds around us,
the music of life.

In the music classroom at Blanton Elementary School in Austin, Texas, this saying was displayed throughout the year on the border above the chalkboard. The letters were cut out of colorful paper, designed to grab the attention of the children. The honored spot among bulletin boards, reserved in most elementary classes for the revered alphabet, was devoted in the music room to a thought about hearing sounds in our world. It reminded the students, and the teacher, that listening is learning to hear and being aware of what we are hearing, and that it is critical to any musical learning because music is the *aural* art. As the alphabet is to words and reading, listening is to sounds and music.

Our world is noisy, and probably as a defense mechanism we learn to mask out sounds. Children learn to focus on the TV show, even though the baby is crying and Mom is on the phone in the kitchen and the stereo is playing rather loudly. This practice of ignoring sound carries into the classroom, where statistics tell us that over half of a child's school day is spent in listening. The teacher who helps students learn to attend aurally is giving them a gift that will foster success throughout their school career, and perhaps throughout their lives. We know that listening plays a key role in communication with others, and certainly it is critical in the learning process.

Focusing on listening will also be of great assistance to the classroom teacher. By teaching children to listen carefully for directions, the elementary classroom teacher can eliminate undue frustrations. The following scenario occurs far too often in the elementary classroom:

> After listing the directions on the board and telling the children what to do, the teacher turns around to see a child whose hand is raised. When recognized, the child asks, "What are we supposed to be doing?" By developing listening skills, children will begin to *hear the first time*, rather than ask those innocent, yet annoying, little questions.

By using music to help children learn to listen more actively and accurately, focus and attention will be sharpened, and the teacher's life will become less frazzled. It is amazing what music can do in the elementary classroom!

TEACHING TIP: Of course, skilled teachers know to involve their students to make sure they hear the directions. Ask one student to recall and state one of the directions. Repeat the question to two other students until all the steps have been remembered and restated. Everyone can give the answer using thumbs up for "yes" and thumbs down for "no." Answer yes or no: Step one is to get out the paper, Step two…etc.

Learning to perform the skill of listening well alleviates many problems for the student and for the teacher. Music, the art form that requires listening, is a perfect conveyance for helping students develop into excellent listeners. Plus, children enjoy listening to music, so they do not perceive it as "work," or something to dread. To them it is fun and excellent teachers know that learning should be enjoyable.

The aural art, music, cultivates the skill of perceptive, involved listening. Teaching children to be active listeners, a gift to be enjoyed for the rest of their lives, is also a classroom activity that all teachers, regardless of talents or skills, can do.
For these reasons, listening is the first musical activity included in this book. Furthermore, it is also a skill intertwined with many of the additional teaching suggestions in the book.

Building audiences is music education

To be able to go to a concert and be transported from the *everyday* by the beauty of music is one of life's special gifts. For a variety of reasons, many people do not take advantage of the gift. Perhaps they feel uneasy at certain types of concerts, or they think they can't relate to some music, or they feel ignorant when they attend a concert where lots of people seem to be enjoying the music but they aren't. All of these valid reasons inhibit concert attendance. Fortunately, the classroom teacher can readily teach the necessary skills.

Some common "fears" about concert attendance countered by the "rules."

FEARS	RULES
I'll clap at the wrong time.	Only clap at the end of compositions or at the end of certain sections of concerts. If unsure, watch the conductor if there is one. When the conductor turns around, it is proper to applaud.
	In vocal concerts, the music is presented in sections, usually grouped according to language. Clap at the end of these sections.
	These rules have developed through the years to help the performers keep their concentration focused on the music.
I won't know what to wear.	Dressing neatly and comfortably is always appropriate. Some people take the opportunity to wear their dressier clothes, but true music lovers pass no judgment on appearance of concertgoers. Those who have attended concerts in Europe know that people there come in all sorts of dress.
I won't know how to act.	Try to be on time, but if traffic or other unavoidable events cause one to be late, wait outside the concert hall door until the end of a composition. Then quietly enter and sit down. If ushers are there, they will help you do this. Again, this is to help the performer(s) concentrate.
	Of course, don't talk during the music. This is very distracting to others in the concert. Follow common behaviors of courtesy, and you will be fine.
I won't like the music.	You won't know unless you go. Enjoying music sometimes requires understanding. It is not an instant attraction for some people.

Read the concert notes to help you prepare for the music. Try to keep your mind focused on the sounds. Often your mind will start to wander because it is relaxing. When that happens, re-attend to what you are hearing.

When you can train yourself to listen attentively to music, it will become a great joy. Why do you think people will drive long distances or go to great lengths just to get to a concert? They have experienced the mind and body "salve" that music affords.

Many school districts offer concert series during the year for students. These sometimes are through an area symphony or through a local college or university. Local high schools have opportunities for elementary students to attend their performances. Some Parent/Teacher groups raise money to bring music events to their schools.

Wise classroom teachers take advantage of these concerts for their students. The most successful ones include some training prior to the event. If your school has a music teacher, this person should be able to help your students learn about the composers and compositions. Check out library books on music, composers, concerts and orchestral instruments to display in the room. Play music during seatwork or reading time or other quiet class times to help students prepare for the concert.

How to get started in teaching students to learn to listen?

Sound-Collecting Walks

The beginning of listening instruction is helping students attend critically to what they are hearing. In our noisy world, this task may be more difficult than first thought. We are bombarded by sounds: on 'hold' on the phone, at the grocery store, in the elevator, in the doctor's office. Some children have to be reminded to take time to listen because they have practiced years of "tuning out" sounds.

Sound-Collecting Walks provide a class activity devoted to listening. It entails capturing sounds on a portable tape recorder as the class or a smaller group walks along listening for sounds in their world.

The walks can be taken outside, taping nature sounds, or throughout the school building locating sounds in the environment of school. Sounds can be collected at sports events, at movies, at picnics, or just about anywhere!

These *Sound-Collecting Walks* can be part of a field trip or a special class outing. Once the tape is made, classify the sounds in various ways – long/short sounds, loud/soft sounds, hi/low sounds, nature-made/man-made sounds, fast/slow sounds, inside sounds/outside sounds. Having the children recognize the opposite nature of some sounds, such as fast as opposed to slow, creates opportunities to begin critical thinking skills. The more refined aspect of listening begins to develop as well. The sound may represent something that is "relatively" fast, but not "extremely" fast.

Students can find or draw pictures to illustrate the sounds. Classroom books can be produced to accompany the sound tape. Large picture books made by the children displayed on a table in the classroom become inviting places to quietly listen and reflect.

Sharing sound tapes with other classes is very entertaining. When no visual image or picture accompanies a sound, deciding what is creating the sound can be quite challenging. A teakettle can sound like a jet plane! The challenge of identifying Mrs. Smith's class tape is great fun for children.

Older children can be assigned to groups, each of which goes on a different *Sound-Collecting Walk*. These tapes can be shared and discussed, and can become the basis of a creative writing assignment or an art experience.

Rule of Three

Music education research provides us a clue for teaching listening successfully. Through research studies we know that repeated listening to a composition produces a more valuable musical experience for the listener. Repetition allows the music to become familiar for the listener who then is more inclined to "like" it. The music becomes a friend or something well known that is pleasurable.

In applying that research to classroom instruction, teaching three planned listening experiences at three different times of the year for each musical composition selected becomes the goal. This suggestion, though different from earlier educational practices, is in agreement with Howard Gardner who advocates that less material be taught more effectively. Teach less better!

Often in school, large amounts of information is covered, but not taught well or effectively, with no emphasis on whether the student has learned it or not. College survey courses devote a semester to this type of instruction. The format includes teacher disseminating much information to grade-oriented students, who then find themselves memorizing the material for a test. After taking the test, and often scoring very well, the students then promptly allow their minds to forget the material because it was not taught or learned effectively.

In much the same way, music teachers were once taught to select for each grade level a larger number of musical compositions that would be listened to once during the year. The **Rule of Three** recommends teaching a fewer number of compositions, but presenting them at three different times in three different lessons.

Suggestions for using the Rule of Three will be given with the recommend listening lessons in this chapter.

Experiences in Listening Starting with Creating

Creating a sound story or composition is an ideal introduction to meaningful listening lessons. Once the children have told a story in sound, they listen with heightened interest and attentiveness to another composer using similar approaches to composing. Programmatic music, music composed to tell a story, is especially effective with this teaching strategy. Children actively listen to Smetana's *The Moldau* or Dukas's *Sorcerer's Apprentice* after they function as composers themselves. Listening lessons hold new meaning because the children can relate to the music as both listeners and composers.

The Moldau
The music of *The Moldau* tells the story of a river, beginning with the tiny tributaries and streams coming together into a mighty moving river. The listener can hear the river deepen as the cellos and low strings begin to play. The story the music tells without words is of a boat floating on the river Moldau, moving past a forest, with passengers observing a group of hunters, and next a wedding party in a Czech village with much celebration and dancing. The music continues the story with the sun setting, and the boat anchoring for the night. The moonlight on the water creates images of nymphs dancing. At the dawning of the new day, the boat continues down the river where a series of dangerous rapids must be crossed. The boat is able to continue on safely through the rapids, arriving in the city of Prague where church bells in the steeples ring out a welcome.

The children can create a composition designed to tell this story in sound.
- They first select sounds to make the water music, beginning very small at first to represent the tributaries. Xylophones played up and down in a glissando work nicely. Start softly on only one instrument, gradually adding more sounds until the river sound is formed.
- Go through the story with the children choosing different sounds to tell the events.
- With no words, tell the story only in sounds.
- Use sentence strips to write each event in the story. Place the strips in a holder.
- As a child points to the strips in the correct order, the other children play the sounds that tell the story.
- When playing the sound composition in this manner, they are following a conductor, just as the orchestra does.
- After they complete their sound story, tell the children that music composed to tell a story is called Programmatic music.
  Someone else has also composed a musical story about this theme.
  Then listen to *The Moldau*, a programmatic composition by Smetana.

By following the **Rule of Three** for listening, myriad possibilities exist. Some weeks or even months later, children could listen a second time to *The Moldau* as they draw their favorite scene from the music which will later become part of a mural for the classroom. A third listening experience could be in relationship to a study of waterways or rivers of the world. (See chapter 7, Science and Music, page 85.) A study of Czechoslovakia would be a perfect time to listen again. Transportation study could motivate another listening to this composition about river travel. Creative writing is always a possibility for the classroom teacher in conjunction with programmatic music. What were the people on the boat doing? Where was their home? Who were the hunters in the forest? Who was being married in the village? What did the boat travelers eat? Where were they going? All these questions can stimulate creative writing experiences for the children.

"Twinkle, Twinkle Little Star" –"Ah, Vous dirai-je, ma-men" by Mozart

A marvelous successful classroom composition activity can be planned using the children's song, "Twinkle, Twinkle Little Star."

- Start with a picture of a star on a poster or sketched on the board. Ask children to name things that come to mind when they see this picture. Teacher lists the words or phrases on the board or overhead as the children state their ideas. Words might include "galaxy," "well done" as in gold star, "sheriff's badge," "movie star" or "Christmas tree."
- Next have the children draw a picture of something having to do with "star." They could draw individually or work in small groups for this part of the project. Discuss their drawings with the whole class when completed.
- Now have the children name songs that have "star" in them. Suggestions probably will include "Star Spangled Banner," "Oh, Little Town of Bethlehem," and of course, "Twinkle, Twinkle Little Star."
- Group the children around bar or keyboard instruments, or have them use recorders if they are learning to play them in music class, or just let them hum the tune. The task is to find the beginning of the "Twinkle" melody. Don't give the answer, but give them time to explore the melody. Usually they can discover the tune:

```
C      C       G     A A     G      F    F     E      E       D     D    C
Twinkle Twinkle Lit-tle Star, How I won-der what you are.
```

- After discovering the melody, have all groups play or sing the tune or "theme" together. Write the word "theme" on the board with the term melody.
- "Now we will create a Theme and Variation on our Twinkle theme." Let the groups explore ways to change or vary their theme. Usually they will explore playing it faster or slower, or changing the rhythm, or letting two people play at the same time with a sort of accompaniment idea. Teacher should wander from group to group, helping them alter and elaborate on their ideas, making it better. Finally, have everyone play the theme together, followed by each group's variation.
- Lastly, let the children listen to Mozart's piano composition, "Ah, Vous dirai-je, ma-men" which is a theme and variation on the tune we recognize as "Twinkle Twinkle Little Star."
- Again, the children will listen with great interest to "another composer's work" of what they have also composed. (This plan also incorporates the Creative Thinking ideas of E. Paul Torrence, see chapter 5, page 64.)

When adhering to the **Rule of Three**, two additional activities should be planned for listening to Mozart's "Ah, Vous dirai-je, ma-men." The students could design listening maps, either in small groups or individually, to use with the composition. They could research facts about the composer Mozart and present a play about his life and work. A timeline showing the age in which Mozart lived could be created, listing scientific discoveries, historical information, and world events that occurred during Mozart's life.

Creative writing and art projects are useful tools in the elementary classroom. The children could write a pretend letter from Mozart to his Mother while he was on tour. What was it like to be a child prodigy? How did it make him feel to perform before the royalty when he was only four years old? What was travel throughout Europe in a stagecoach like for a young boy? Scenes from Mozart's life and times could become artworks to decorate the classroom. What were the clothes like? Compare today's clothes with those worn by Mozart? How would he like to wear jeans?

L'Histoire du Soldat-**by Stravinsky and**
"The Devil Went Down to Georgia"—Charlie Daniels

Historical Background:
L'Histoire du Soldat, a composition by Igor Stravinsky, makes a great compose-it-first, then listen activity. Stravinsky created this work for two dancers, a narrator, and a very unusual instrumentation including a cornet, a bassoon, and a string bass. He wrote the work while living in Paris after he left Russia at the beginning of the revolution leading to Communism in the early 2oth century. During this time in history many artists escaped Russia due to the restrictive environment imposed by the communist regime that was void of the personal freedoms many artists require to create. Stravinsky had friends who could perform in this work, and they could travel easily around Paris performing and earning badly needed financial remuneration. Stravinsky chose a tale that many artists have used as the theme of the musical work.

The Story:
The story goes something like this. A young soldier is in love and engaged to a young woman living in his home village. He is away in the army, but has vacation or leave, so he starts out to see his fiancée. While he is walking to the village, he sits down to rest in the woods and takes out his violin to play. The soldier loves the violin, and plays with ease and with great enjoyment. Suddenly, out of the woods appears an evil looking man who wants to buy his violin. The soldier responds "NO." The violin is much too important to him to sell it, and besides he wants to continue to play.

The evil man suggests they have a contest, with the better player winning the violin. The soldier agrees to this ill-fated contest, and loses the challenge. The evil man disappears into the forest with the violin in his hand. Following this event, the soldier becomes disoriented and wanders aimlessly without even knowing what he is doing. The fiancée knows that something terrible has happened to her lover, perhaps even death.

Finally, the soldier does make his way to the village and reunites with his fiancée. He explains to her the horrible contest and how much he realizes the violin meant to him. It is very important to his life, almost like a representation of his soul. He vows to find the evil man and have another contest, which he does. This time, the soldier, full of newfound determination and self-will wins the violin back.

This tale can be the basis of a grand musical experience for the children. A Friday afternoon provides the perfect time to devote for this listening adventure as children explore the process of creativity.

- Tell the children the story of the soldier and his violin. If a small violin can be found, even one that is a Christmas tree ornament, use it as a visual prop.
- Borrow percussion instruments from the music class and have the children compose music to fit the story. Music will be needed for the soldier, his walk in the forest, the evil man, the fiancée, the contests, and any other sounds the children think fit.
- All the students should be involved.
- Tell the story again, in abbreviated form, with the children playing their created music as accompaniment.
- Then have the music tell the story without words. At this step, the different parts to the composition should be listed on the board or on sentence strips in a holder. Teacher can point to the words to help keep the performers "on track." Teacher may need to pantomime or suggest with movements or mouthed words the different characters and parts of the story to help keep the momentum of the creative play.

The resulting programmatic composition can be taped and reviewed by the students who evaluate the success of their creation. Asking questions such as "Can we make it better?" or "Did you find any parts that we need to revise?" focus the students on the task of evaluation.

As a final step, listen to portions of Stravinsky's composition, *L'Histoire du Soldat*. They will hear typical Stravinsky-ish syncopation and jagged rhythms, and his use of the dissonant and unusual in melody and harmony.

By this time, some child has probably mentioned another composition that has many of the same ideas as the Stravinsky. The more recent popular country western song, "The Devil Went Down to Georgia," by Charlie Daniels tells the same type of story, only this time it is a Georgia boy who has a contest with the devil. Use the accompanying music map to listen now to this composition.

Again, by first exploring their own creative abilities, the children are much more interested in listening to another's similar composition. This lesson adapts easily to the **Rule of Three**. Other listenings might include a study of the history of Russian communism, or research on Stravinsky as one of the premiere 20th century composers, or reports on the cold war or time lines developed to show the early 1900s as to scientific and creative discoveries: any topic that leads to an additional listening experience of *L'Histoire du Soldat* will serve well.

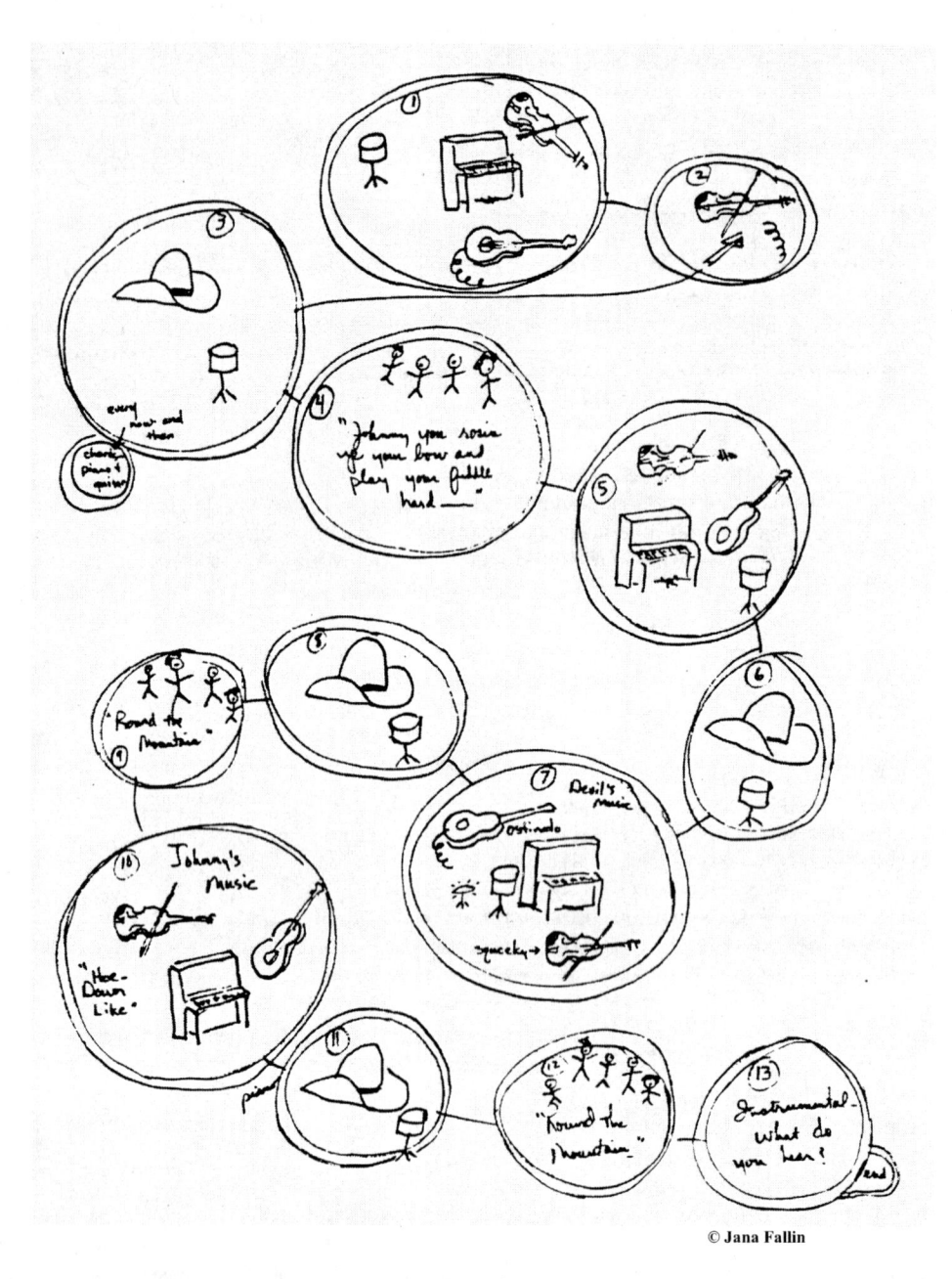

**Listening Map
"Devil Went Down to Georgia"
Charlie Daniels**

© Jana Fallin

Experiences in Listening using Children's Books

Swanlake, adapted by Rachel Isadora, tells the story of the ballet. If the students read this book in class, listening to selections of Tchaikovsky's music will enrich the reading experience. *The Nutcracker* has been published by Peter Spier as a storybook and also can be found as an Advent calendar that can serve as a clever introduction to the ballet. The calendar holds twenty tiny books telling the story. Children could read the story before listening to the music. The **Rule of Three** could be followed with a video clip of these ballets. Again, art and creative writing are always possibilities for the classroom teacher. A study of the composer who was rather bizarre will be interesting for the students. He thought his head was going to blow off his body, so he conducted his music with one hand as he held on to his head with the other hand. The accompanying listening map and music found on the CD is very helpful in teaching the form of the Nutcracker "March."

Prokofiev's *Peter and the Wolf* has been designed and illustrated as a book by Warren Chappell. The pictures, with musical themes included, make the story come alive for students. Supplying the visual to accompany the aural experience provides a more successful listening event for many children. Puppets made from small brown paper sacks or from drawings by the children attached to craft sticks (Have sketches in the margin.) can be used to tell the story.

Discovering the Art of Music

Good art has three qualities:

Unity   **Variety**   **Balance**

Listening to a wide range of music helps students discover these qualities in compositions. Throughout the year, students can apply these standards to music and art. Their art criticism skills will be honed, and they will know why they like or dislike a certain piece of music. The ability to discuss both verbally and in writing the qualities of music should be evident. Additionally, because they are using higher level thinking skills of comparison and contrast, these music exercises are good for their brains; much like aerobic exercise is good for the body.

The "Hallelujah Chorus" from Handel's *Messiah* is an excellent example of unity, variety and balance in music. This classic work of art from the Baroque period of music history (See timeline on page 41.) is part of the oratorio *Messiah*. An oratorio is a large work for orchestra, chorus and soloists, usually on a religious theme.

- In the beginning of the chorus, the voices are singing in four part harmony. Handel then has the voices singing in unison (all the same melody line), interestingly as the contour of the melody suggests a large "M." Then, he has the voices return to their four-part singing. This planned part of the composition creates variety, unity and balance for the listener. Even when we are not cognizant of this feature, our ears are pleased with the sounds.

- Continuing on with the composition, we find a section starting with the text "The kingdom of this world is become...." which is very smooth in sound, creating great variety from the more jagged feeling of the music heard previously.
- The fugal section begins with the words "And he shall reign" starting with the basses, followed by tenors, then altos and last by the sopranos. This section is a sort of "follow the leader" design. Again, variety within the composition, yet balanced by the similar lengths of the music sung by each voice part.

When asked if this composition may be included in the curriculum of a public school in the United States, some elementary education majors often answer "no." This misguided interpretation of following the laws of Separation of Church and State within the public schools is unfortunately quite common. However, teaching a classic work of art as a music education experience is completely within the law.

As you read previously in the discussion of the "Hallelujah Chorus," the composition was discussed musically as to the inclusion of the qualities of unity, variety and balance. The selection could also have been taught emphasizing musical elements such as tone color or melodic treatment, or through a study of instrumentation, or by examples of repetition/contrast or from a variety of other musical features. The "Hallelujah Chorus" was chosen as an example of a great work of art, not as a religious or doctrinal lesson, and is therefore a legal as well as an educationally sound inclusion for a listening event.

Listening to several versions of the same musical composition

Comparing two or more versions of the same piece of music can be a very captivating listening lesson for the elementary age student. By having students listen to one selection and then to a second piece and compare and contrast the two, higher level thinking skills are required.

"Star Spangled Banner"

Many versions of the National Anthem are available, and provide a perfect segue into patriot music unit or a study of early American history. Listening to a version played by a wind ensemble, a vocal version sung by Sandi Patty, and the electric guitar version played by Jimi Hendricks at Woodstock give very different feelings for the listener. A chart listing 'Same --- Different' (see attached forms) for each of the versions can be given to students, to be completed either individually or in small groups. Discussing points of the compositions that are the same and what makes them different is an analysis skill requiring students to mentally compare and contrast what they heard. Questions of which version was the favorite involves evaluation, another higher level thinking skill.

"Flight of the BumbleBee"

"Flight of the BumbleBee" is available in several versions. The original version is from *Tale of the Tsar Salton* and many versions exist with trumpet solos. Doc Sverensen plays one trumpet version with the Cincinnati Pops Orchestra, and the Canadian Brass also have a version performed totally by brass instruments. YoYo Ma and Bobby McFerren, on their CD *Hush*, have a recording of "Flight of the BumbleBee" which is played by voice and cello. All these selections can be contrasted or two versions can be selected for comparison, helping elementary children improve their listening perception.

"Danny Boy"
The Irish folk song "Danny Boy" provides many examples for listening to a variety of versions. Percy Grainger's *Lincolnshire Posey* uses the folk tune as a theme, and many contemporary groups including the Chieftains have recorded it. Also, vocalists through the years have sung "Danny Boy," including opera voices and country singers. Ray Price, a C&W artist, performed "Danny Boy" with strings and created quite a furor among country western audiences who felt he had left his roots by adding orchestral strings to a country music recording.

"Somewhere" from West Side Story
Voices as distinctive as Barbara Streisand and Placido Domingo have recordings of this solo from the musical *West Side Story*. Some children will not perceive that the two songs are the same because a man is singing one and a woman the other, where some children will have trouble listing as a difference that one is a male voice and one is female. Exploring different versions of a composition provides an entertaining respite during the school day. Watching as the children respond to the lesson and listening to their comments gives a teacher new insights into his or her students.

Forms to use with listening to two versions of the same song are in the appendices.

Listening through the Historical Periods

Baroque:

Bach: *Little Fugue in g*

Handel: "Hallelujah Chorus" from the *Messiah*

Classical:

Mozart: "Twinkle, Twinkle Little Star" – "Ah, Vous dirai-je, ma-men"

Haydn: *Surprise Symphony*

Beethoven: *Symphony No. 5*
Symphony No. 9
(Beethoven is such a pivotal composer that he spans the Classical into the Romantic Historic Periods)

Romantic:

Tchaikovsky: *Nutcracker Ballet*

Mussorgsky: "Ballet of Unhatched Chicks" from *Pictures at an Exhibition*

Impressionism:

Debussy: "Golliwog's Cakewalk" from *Children's Corner*

Debussy: *Prelude to the Afternoon of a Faun*

Ravel: *Bolero*

Modern:

Aaron Copland: "Walk to the Bunkhouse" from *Red Pony Suite*

Aaron Copland: "Simple Gifts" from *Appalachian Spring*

Ferde Grofe: "On the Trail" from *Grand Canyon Suite*

Gould: *American Salute*

Benjamin Britten: *Young Person's Guide to the Orchestra*

Stravinsky: *L'Histoire du Soldat* with Charlie Daniel's "Devil Went Down to Georgia"

Using Listening Maps to Teach

The following "maps" are visual representation of music. They are designed to help children perceive aurally (listen) more effectively. The teacher should make an overhead transparency and follow along on the map as the children watch and listen. The goal is to listen without talking at all. The only sound that should be heard is the music, which allows the children to focus all their "ear attention" on the music . The first map is for "On the Trail" from Grand Canyon Suite by Ferde Grofe. The second map is for use with "If You're Going to Play in Texas," by the popular group, Alabama.

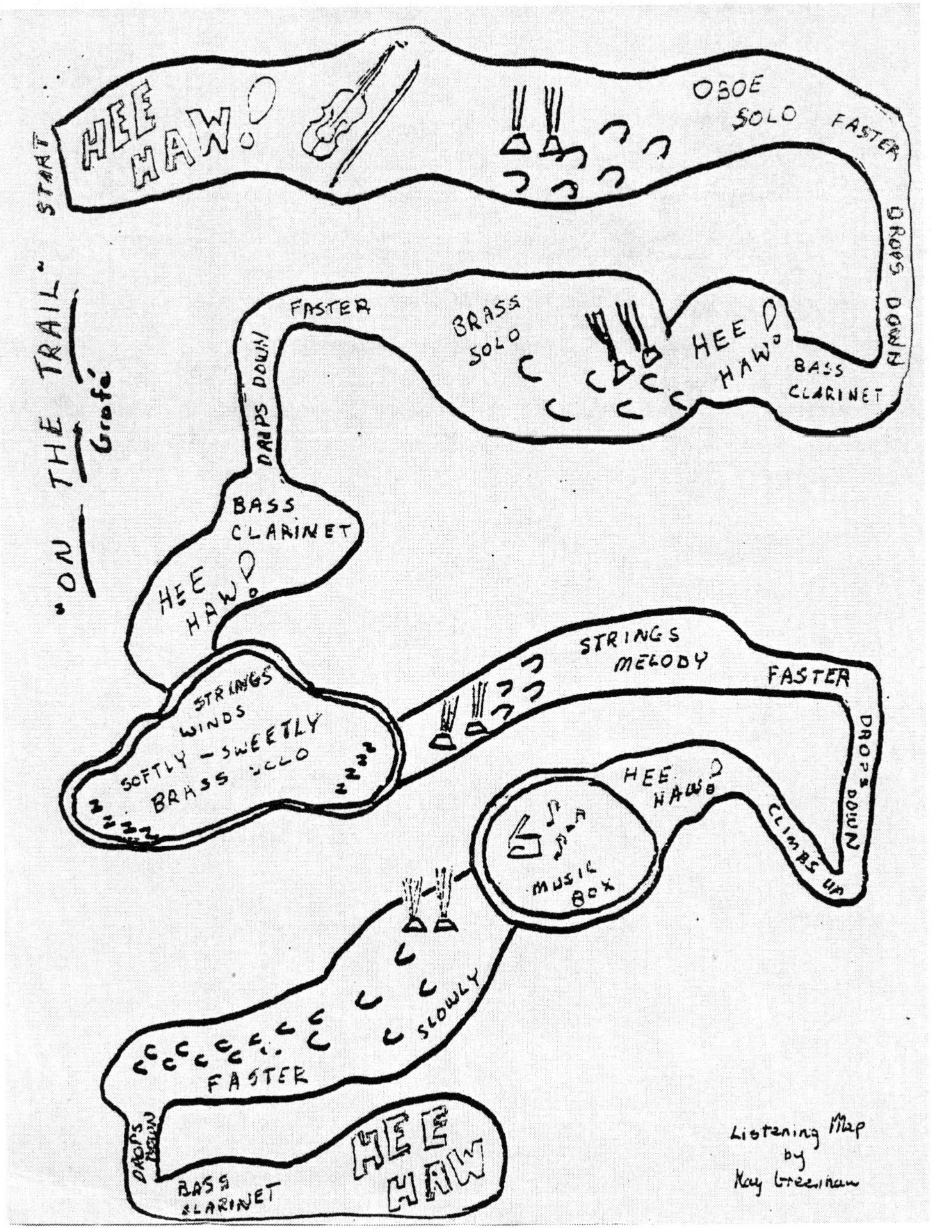
"ON THE TRAIL"
Grofé
START
HEE HAW
OBOE SOLO
FASTER
DROPS DOWN
BASS CLARINET
HEE HAW
BRASS SOLO
FASTER
DROPS DOWN
BASS CLARINET
HEE HAW
STRINGS WINDS
SOFTLY - SWEETLY
BRASS SOLO
STRINGS MELODY
FASTER
DROPS DOWN
CLIMBS UP
HEE HAW
MUSIC BOX
SLOWLY
FASTER
DROPS DOWN
BASS CLARINET
HEE HAW
Listening Map by Kay Greenhaw

Introduction

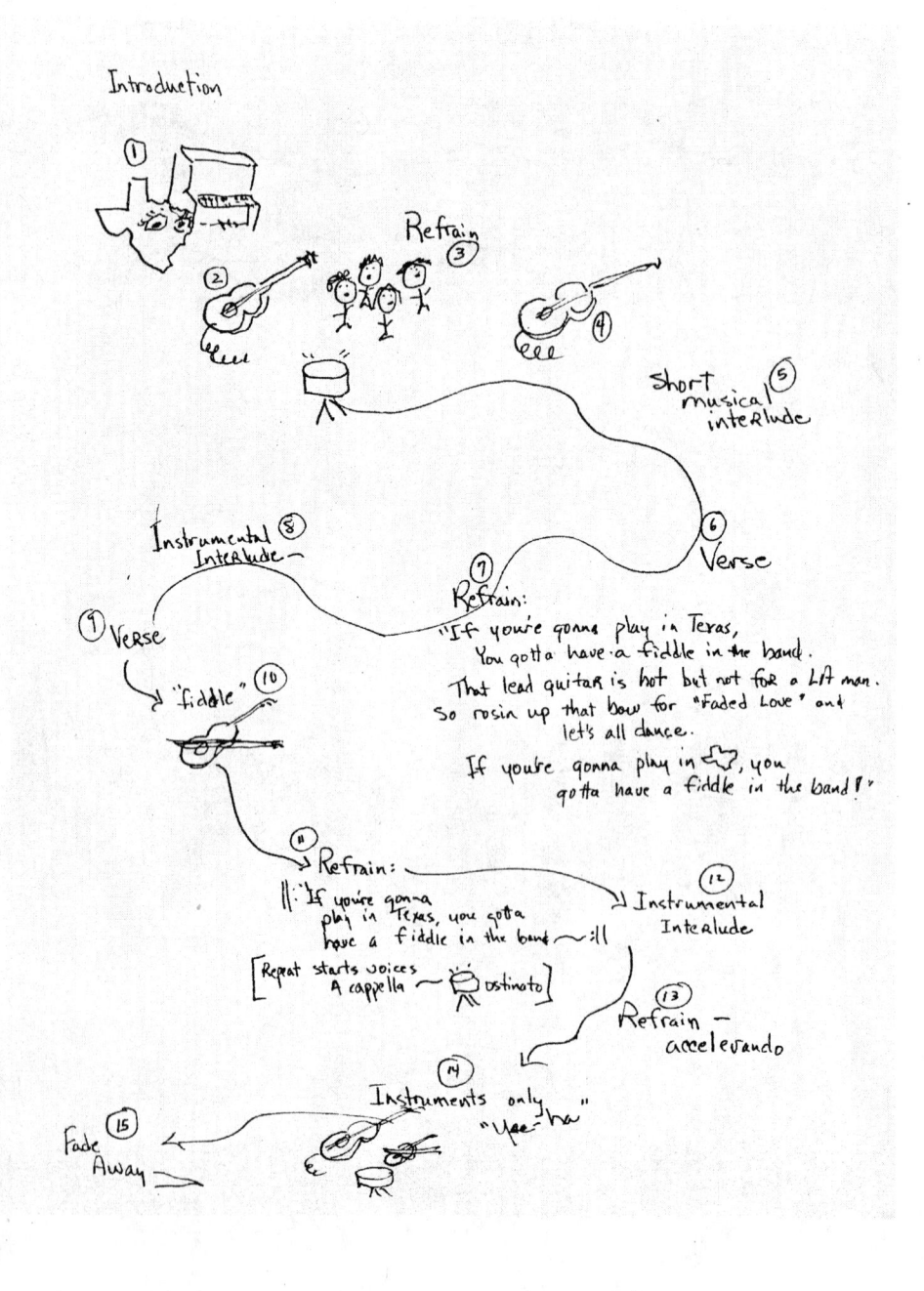

① [Texas/piano sketch]

② [guitar] Refrain ③ [people singing] ④ [fiddle]

⑤ Short musical interlude

⑥ Verse

⑧ Instrumental Interlude

⑦ Refrain:
"If you're gonna play in Texas,
You gotta have a fiddle in the band.
That lead guitar is hot but not for a LA man.
So rosin up that bow for "Faded Love" and
let's all dance.
If you're gonna play in [Texas], you
gotta have a fiddle in the band!"

⑨ Verse

→ "fiddle" ⑩

⑪ Refrain:
"If you're gonna play in Texas, you gotta have a fiddle in the band" ~ill

[Repeat starts voices A cappella ~ ostinato]

⑫ Instrumental Interlude

⑬ Refrain — accelerando

⑭ Instruments only "Yee-ha"

Fade ⑮ Away

Chapter 4
Performing
Singing   Playing   Moving

One of the most important components in teaching music to children is to help them become performers of music. When thinking of the word "perform," most probably think of professional musicians who make their livelihood through singing on a stage to large audiences and by producing CDs of their music to sell.

Performing can also be done in the classroom, with little polishing. Children will be very willing to perform for their teacher and for each other. It is a sharing of music with one another.

Singing, Playing and Moving are musical performance activities.

Singing
The fortunate person is one who enjoys singing. Many people go through life thinking they are incapable of singing in tune. Research is full of studies showing that anyone, if they have no vocal damage or disabling hearing condition, can learn to match pitch and sing.

"Well, they haven't heard me," is an almost audible response to these research findings because many people feel they cannot sing. If a person is able to yell at someone in the parking lot and their voice naturally moves up and down a bit, and their hearing is normal, they can learn to sing.

Of course, it is easier to teach singing to a young child who has not experienced the harsh, negative statements from teachers, family, or peers criticizing the singing voice. But remember the research, ANYONE CAN LEARN TO SING. If one wants to sing, they can learn. Deciding to do it is the beginning step. Singing in the shower, singing to the radio, singing at church are all good activities in developing a singing voice.

Helping children find and use their singing voice is something the classroom teacher can do. The children are relaxed with their teacher, they trust that this person is not going to do something embarrassing to them, and singing together builds community. Plus, the principal will be thrilled, the music teacher will be grateful, and the children will be able to sing the "Star Spangled Banner" at ballgames without feeling embarrassed. What a gift to give.

Matching Pitch
Helping children match pitch can be achieved through classroom activities.

- Call roll by singing. Teacher sings the child's name on the pitches Sol Mi. The child sings the response, "I'm here" using the same pitches.
- As the children get better at matching pitch, try changing the pitch levels. Move the Sol Mi higher or lower to see if the child can match the pitch.
- A teacher who consistently uses this activity through the school year will have children matching pitch by the end of the year.
- Always encourage them honestly. "You're getting better," or "You are going to learn this" are statements that help children feel like they can do it!

Use the "Natural Chant of Childhood" to teach tone matching.
Children taunting on the playground are singing these sounds called the "Natural Chant of Childhood." "Johnny is a sissy," or "Nanny Nanny Boo Boo" are sung on this series of pitches. Listening to children at recess time will almost always result in hearing some child or group of children singing these pitches. No one teaches them either, yet every generation of children will know this little tune.

The tones are actually:

sol   sol   mi   la   sol   mi

Using these tones that are naturally easy for most children to sing will help with tone matching. Playing singing games using the "Natural Chant of Childhood" is good practice for singing.

- Singing for students to line up. "Let's line up for lunch time" sung to the "Natural Chant of Childhood" or to the tune of "99 Bottles of Beer on the Wall" will work. "Are you sleeping" and "Skip to my Lou" work also. The song might go something like this:
  > Let's line up for lunch time,
  > Let's line up right now.
  > What a great group of children I see,
  > Lining up for chow!
- Make up the words impromptu, the sillier the better, and the children will be laughing and singing, just for the fun of it! They don't know that you are helping them learn to match pitch.
- Making up little songs for recess, for library, for almost anything the children are to do is good.
- Sing when it is time to pick up before the end of the day. Everyone will feel much better doing it this way rather than teacher nagging the children to gather up their belongings and put away their books.
- As the teacher begins to sing, the children can join in with a light, lovely singing voice as they line up to leave the room.

Almost any nursery rhyme or poem can be sung to the tune of "99 Bottles of Beer on the Wall," according to Laurie Curtis, who is known as the 'singing teacher' because she has sung to children in her classroom for many years. She attributes much of her success as a teacher to using music to help children learn more effectively.

A fun singing game using a basketball or other large ball can be sung to the "99 Bottles" tune. Children are in a circle, and one child starts bouncing the ball to another child. The whole group sings the song "Bounce High Bounce Low, Bounce the Ball to Jericho, Bounce High Bounce Low." The child tossing the ball sings "Bounce the Ball to Ben," (singing the name of the child who received the ball). Then Ben chooses a child, and tosses the ball to the new player. Again, the whole group sings until the line where the "tosser" sings alone. After a child has tossed the ball, he/she sits down, but continues to sing with the group. Children sit down and keep singing after having their turn so that the class can easily see who is left to call on. This game is fun, helps children learn the names of their classmates, and gives practice on singing alone and with others, which is the first standard in the National Standards of Music.

> Bounce High, Bounce Low,
> Bounce the ball to Jericho
> Bounce High, Bounce Low,
> Bounce the ball to (a child's name)

Helping the Child Who Is Not Yet Matching Pitch
If a child cannot match pitch at all, and seems to "growl" the sounds on a low pitch, they perhaps haven't discovered how it feels to move the voice. Playing games that require making sounds can be the magic combination for certain children.
- Getting them to make the sound of a siren, starting with a low sound, going higher, then back to a low sound can get a child used to moving the voice.
- Have all the children do the "game" together because the emerging singer doesn't need to feel singled out. Plus the other children will want to do the game.
- Start with their bodies in a kneeling position close to the ground, hands on the floor. As they make the sound of the siren, and the sound goes up, the children stand up and stretch their arms high.
- Return to the low position as the pretend siren comes back down.

Things to Remember:

> If a child can "holler" to a friend on the playground and it sounds normal, the child is not a monotone.

> Keep telling them they can learn. Believing it can happen is an important part of this struggle.

Boys match pitch later than girls. Even as late as 4th grade, some boys are just beginning to match pitch.

The mind is a powerful tool, and believing is a very important part of learning. Teachers are sometimes like doctors who need to convince their patients that a cure is possible. Believing that one will get well is important to medical cures, and the same is true in learning. Help them "believe" they can learn by saying, "You're going to get it." This is a true statement, because the research has proven that people can learn to sing.

Selecting Songs to Sing

Many sources are available for songs appropriate for the elementary student. Some collections, available in children's bookstores, are noteworthy.

> *Gonna Sing My Head Off*
> *Laura Ingalls Wilder Song Book*
> *The Book of Childrens Songtales*

Professional recordings for singing along can be remarkable assets to the classroom teacher. (Warning: Some recordings are pitched too low for the children. If it is more chant-like or sung like a cheerleader, the music is probably too low. Look for music from middle c to the c above, especially around f or g up to c.)

Recordings for the classroom music series from MacMillan, Warner Brothers and Silver Burdett are available. Asking the music teacher to make a tape of the children's favorite songs will be especially popular. The music teacher will be thrilled that a classroom teacher is singing with her children, and the children will be thrilled because they are getting to sing their favorite songs outside of music class.

The Wee Sing series available at bookstores, educational supplies and discount stores are helpful. Some of the Disney Sing-Along tapes and videos are fun to use with elementary children.

Playing

Putting an instrument in a child's hand can be all the motivation needed to get even the shyest child involved. Drums, triangles, woodblocks, tone blocks...all the instruments from our memory of elementary school will work. Also, "found sounds" can be instruments. Tapping the side of the desk with a pencil or shaking a *Pringle* potato chip can with a few pebbles or rice or beans inside are also instruments.

One warning! DO NOT let this be the scenario in your classroom.
A box is sitting on the floor filled with random instruments which appear to have been haphazardly thrown in. It is music time, and children come to the box and grab one instrument to "play" while teacher puts on a musical tape or CD. They end up "beating the tar out" of the instruments with this wild sound erupting from the room. They usually are "playing" their instruments whether the music is playing or not. It is difficult to get them to put the instruments back in the box. Discipline is on the verge of dissipating into chaos.

Such bedlam is not music, but it is a scene often found when visiting classrooms, especially with very young children.

Direct playing instruments through games and activities that will increase children's motor skills and reading skills, and also will help them learn to play more musically.

Approaches for Playing

1st Charts can be made or purchased which have rhythms to play.
The Mary Helen Richards Threshold to Music charts are wonderful examples of good charts. Using these charts helps children learn to read music, and to read words as well. The children can clap or play a percussion instrument on the rhythms. By reading the charts, which can be performed successfully by most children, they also learn left to right directionality. As students read one line, at the end they return to the beginning of the next line, thus they are practicing an important component of learning to read.

The Richards charts start with pictures, which are read left to right. Gradually the symbol | (ta) is added to the words. Eventually, the beat is divided and the symbol ⊓ (tee tee) is learned. These symbols will become the quarter note and the eighth note in actual musical notation.

Teachers can also design original charts. Usually, charts are in three lines, with four beats per line. Putting these pictures on large charts allows the children to come up and point to the pictures as the other children say it. Be sure they keep a steady beat while they read. Teacher can say, "One, Two, Ready Go," with a steady beat and then have the children join in. An example of a teacher-made chart would be:

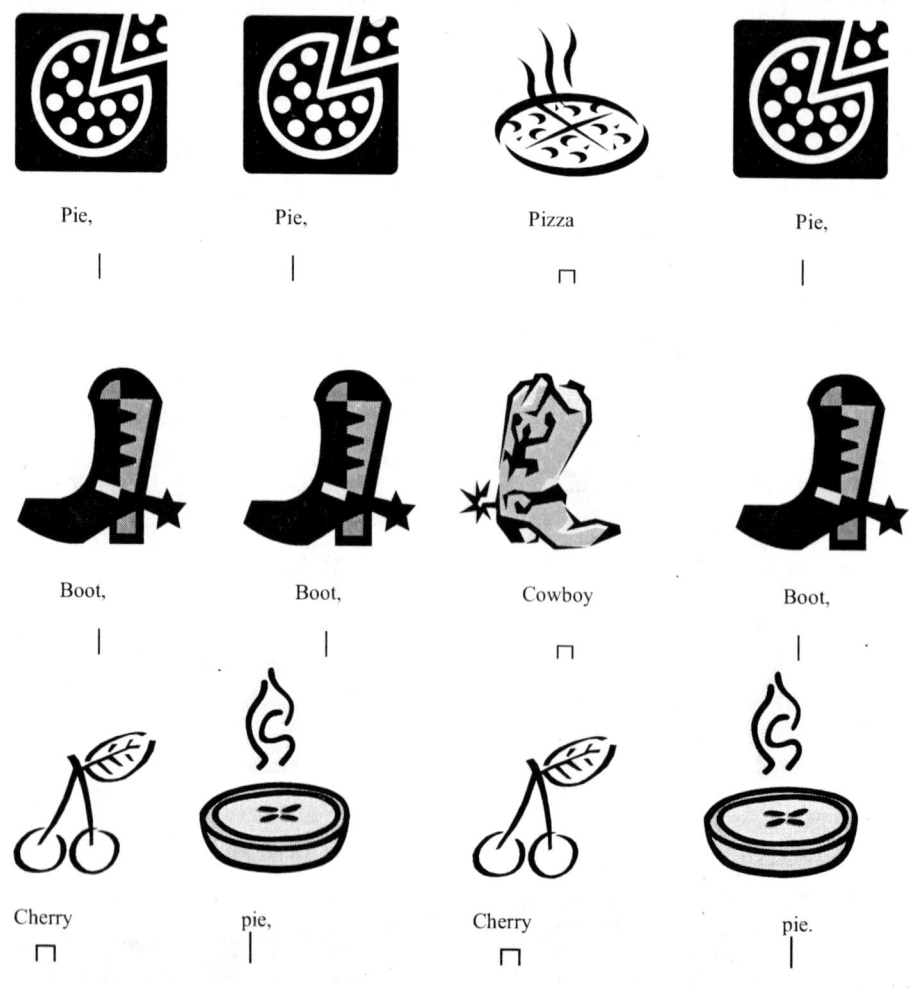

Pie,	Pie,	Pizza	Pie,
|	|	⊓	|
Boot,	Boot,	Cowboy	Boot,
|	|	⊓	|
Cherry	pie,	Cherry	pie.
⊓	|	⊓	|

The next step would be to pick instruments to play on the words, rather than say the words. Children are reading and performing from a score when they do this activity.

2nd   Chants and Nursery Rhymes can be "Played."

Horse and a Flea and three blind mice,

Sat on a curbstone shooting dice,

Horse he turned and sat on the flea,

"Oops" said the flea, "There's a horse on me!"

As a group, say the poem rhythmically. Then the poem can be performed using body sounds which will be transferred to instrument sounds. Children again are performing from a score.

- Have the children select one or two words in each line and draw a circle around them.
- Say the poem snapping the circled words.
- Do the same thing with one or two different words, this time drawing squares around the words.
- Say the poem, snapping circled words and clapping on squared words.
- Children pick a phrase to underline.
- Say the poem, snapping and clapping and adding pats on the knees on the underlined parts.
- Say the poem, doing all the above.
- Now "say" the poem using only the body sounds. For success, everyone "mouth" the words, but don't say them. By only doing the body sounds on the appropriate words, you have a sound composition.
- Next have them select instruments to substitute for the body-part sounds. A hand drum could play the squared words, a triangle on the circled words, temple blocks on the underlined parts, or whatever the children want to select. (Borrow instruments from the music room, or use found sounds from the room or home.)
- Say the poem as a group, adding the instruments on the appropriate words. Then play the "composition", mouthing the words, having only the instruments making sounds.
- Do an ABA composition, instrument sounds only on A, and body sounds only on B. Any combination of sounds can be created. Children arranged in groups can decide what ABA form they choose to perform.
- Adding an ostinato, which plays throughout the composition, tends to make the creative experience more musical and cohesive.
- Inserting an introduction and a coda, or ending, also adds to the musical experience.

Categorize sounds
Organize instruments into the following categories of sounds:

Click	tone blocks, rhythm sticks
Jingle	sleigh bells, tambourines
Rattle	maracas
Scrape	guirro
Ring	finger cymbals, triangle
Membranic	drums

After categorizing the sounds, create a rhythmic composition with the class, using the ta | and tee-tee ⊓ from the charts. Designate which sounds will play the different rhythms. Pictures or color-coding (rattles are red, clicks are green, etc.) can indicate which instrument plays where. Children draw the rhythms with different colored markers, which direct children holding certain instruments when to play. It is like reading a code, and the mind becomes actively involved in this performance game.

Grids
Children are directed to place two beats in each box on the grid. All the boxes must be different. Once the boxes are filled, read the grid from left to right. Then read it 'bingo style', diagonally, in reverse. Play instruments, assigning one instrument to each line.

African Rhythms

Have a line of 12 beats

        1 2 3 4 5 6 7 8 9 10 11 12

Make up patterns using the 12 beat line.

        1 - - 4 - - 7 - - 10 - -

Children clap only on the numbers left in the pattern.

Create a group of these lines.

        - 2 3 - 5 6 - 8 9 - 11 12

        1 2 - - 5 6 - - 9 10 - -

        1 - 3 - 5 - 7 - 9 - 11 -

        1 2 3 - 5 6 7 - 9 10 11 -

        - 2 - 4 5 - 7 - 9 10 - 12

Assign different instruments for each line. Have a drum keep the steady beat. Layer the different instruments in, playing repeatedly the same line.
Get all the instruments playing the different patterns at the same time and it sounds much like African drumming patterns. This creates a fascinating *carpet of sound*, and can be a delightful accompaniment to the reading of African poems.

Native American Stories
Tell the following story to the children:

> Once a little boy named Red Fox lived out on the prairie with his family.
> His father, a chief named Black Horse, was concerned that Red Fox would ride his pony away from the village and need help, but would be unable to call loudly enough. The father decided to use drums to keep in touch with Red Fox during the day, rather like we use cellular phones in today's world.

When Black Horse took his drum, a large drum, he would beat the following rhythm:

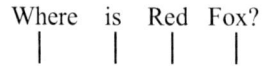

> Where is Red Fox?
> | | | |

When Red Fox heard the drum, he would answer,

> Here I am, Here I am.
> ⊓ | ⊓ |

If Red Fox got in trouble and needed help, he was to tap on his drum

> Come Father! Come Father!
> | ⊓ | ⊓

One day Red Fox rode his pony out to the creek bed and started up a steep hill. While he was riding up the hill, the pony's hooves started to slip, and the little rocks on the path were sliding down causing the boy and the horse to be in a very dangerous spot. Red Fox quickly grabbed his drum, a small drum he kept with him at all times, and tapped:

> Come Father! Come Father!

Black Horse was in the village working when he heard the drum beat out Red Fox's cry for help. The Chief immediately snatched his drum from the ground by his teepee and ran toward to creek bed from where the sounds were coming. Black Horse beat on his drum:

> Where is Red Fox?

Red Fox heard the father's drum and beat the answer:

> Here I am! Here I am!

The Chief and his son were able to find each other by using their drum language, and children in the classroom can do the same. Give one child a smaller drum (it could be handmade from an oatmeal box.) and another child a drum with a different sound. The first child hides somewhere in the school, and starts the drum talk. The second student must find the first with only the drum talk. No vocal talking allowed!

Moving

Moving to music is a natural expression for children. Once with a group of third graders, the children were moving only certain body parts while listening to a very rhythmic arrangement of "Candy Man." "Move only your hands," directed the teacher, while she encouraged the children to think of different ways to move their hands to the music. The activity continued as the teacher would direct, "Move your hips" or knees or elbows or ears…the more outrageous the better because it forces them to think creatively. As the game was going along, with the teacher continuing to suggest different body parts to move, one little girl named Mary Louise urgently requested in a loud voice, "Let my feet go, Let my feet go, Miss Rudolph!" It was not normal behavior for Mary Louise to shout out in class, as she was a rather quiet, reserved child. In class that day she was experiencing the joy of moving to music, and she was so involved in the lesson that she "forgot" the rules of the classroom---raise your hand if you want to say something. This delightful activity was so all encompassing to her body, mind, and spirit that she felt compelled to shout out her desire to "let go!" This out-of-character experience for my little curly-headed Mary Louise remains one of my favorite memories of teaching elementary school music.

The teacher does not have to be Fred Astaire or wear a leotard and tights with ballet slippers to include movement in the classroom. Using these "tried and true" games will work. Applying the label "game" is sometimes more successful for some children than the term "dance." Some teachers try games where the students do not hold hands with one another for beginning experiences, and that proves successful, too.

Drums
1. Take a drum (borrow it from the music teacher or make one out of a coffee can) and play a steady beat. Have the children walk to the beat. Try to match the natural speed of the children with your beat.

> This is a locomotor movement. Locomotor movements include walking, skipping, running, trotting, tiptoeing, and gliding: any movement that goes somewhere. Think of a train locomotive moving down the track.

2. Play two drums of differing sizes, one with a higher pitch, for this game. Tap a steady beat on the lower drum and the children walk with bent knees. Tap a steady beat on the higher pitched drum, and children tiptoe to the beat. Alternate the sounds so the children must respond with their body as to what they are hearing.

        Low Low   Low   Low

        High High   High   High

Mix up the patterns such as High Low Low
High Low Low

3. If you have a drum with a metal part attaching the drumhead onto the wooden body of the drum, play a steady beat on the drumhead and then tap the metal part in a steady beat, alternating wood and metal sounds. The children walk forward to the drumhead sound, and backwards to the metal sound. They can also decide on different ways to walk to the metal sound. Sideways, in a circle, with a partner, or whatever they decide can work.

Teaching Tip

These are wonderful activities to fill in between lessons. When changing from math to reading time during the day, do one of these movement games. The change-of-pace activity brings a refreshing atmosphere in the class and the children. The result for learning is rather amazing as well. The word Recreation can be read Re-Creation. Using movement games as "filler" activities helps the children re-create their attitudes and motivation for learning.

Also, this practice of using "filler" games keeps the amount of on-task time in the classroom especially high. Some classrooms are filled with dead time---when the students are sharpening pencils, when they are getting out books, when they are lining up at the door to go outside. Making transitions into learning experiences by using movement games keeps the motivation elevated and maintains order in the classroom.

Sounds for Movement

Not all movement has to be done with a drum. You can use a variety of games including movement, some of which require very little space in the classroom.

Find a metal sound such as a cymbal or triangle or lid to a pot that when hit keeps on sounding. Have the children stand and "plant their feet" like trees with roots. Play the metal sound, and the children are directed to keep moving as long as the sound is heard.

They can use arms, bend at the waist, twist the body, but the key to this movement game is to keep the feet from moving yet somehow keep the body moving as long as the sound is heard.

> This movement is called a non-locomotor movement. Bending, swaying, twisting, reaching, and stretching are all examples. Non-locomotor movements do not move the body from one spot to another.

Teaching Tip

With movement activities, children may have to be taught to respond without "going wild." Often, they have been so rigid in school that any freedom is taken to the extremes. Learning self-discipline is an important life-skill, and these games can promote children becoming self-disciplined learners.

Children like these movement games, so setting the rules and keeping them will help maintain order in class. Having children "find their own space," not touching anyone will offer a good start. If a child disobeys, he/she sits down. No one wants to "sit" while the others are having fun.

Movement Games

- Mirroring is fun for children. Children face a partner and decide which of the two will be the leader. When teacher plays the cymbal, the leader of the pair moves while the sound is heard, and the partner follows the leader, as in a mirror. After a few times moving to the sound, switch leaders. The rule is they have to remain in their small space, as though facing a mirror that remains stationary. Otherwise you will have children scurrying all around the room trying to copy their leader's movements.

- Walking the beat of a poem is great fun. Tap the steady beat on an instrument such as a woodblock. After the students get good at walking the beat, have them "freeze" when the sound stops. Read the poem and tap the beat, stopping at unusual spots. The children must stop when the sound stops.

- Using poems such as "New Shoes" for movement games with children is also fun. Buying shoes is such a part of a child's life and an important activity for a child when entering school. They easily relate to this poem.

>   New Shoes, New Shoes,
>   Red and pink and blue shoes,
>   Which ones would you choose
>   If you could buy?

It is also fascinating for children to listen to the sound made by different shoes. Sit in a circle, let one child be "it" and walk around the outside of the circle while the students quietly say the poem, listening to the sounds of the shoes. Leather soles will make different sounds from rubber-soled shoes; sandals will produce a unique sound, as will flip-flops.

Old favorites like "Teddy Bear, Teddy Bear" and other jump-rope chants are good resources for movement games.

>	Teddy Bear, Teddy Bear, Turn Around,
>	Teddy Bear, Teddy Bear, Touch the Ground.
>
>	Teddy Bear, Teddy Bear, Hands up high,
>	Teddy Bear, Teddy Bear, Reach the sky.

- A popular game for elementary-age children is called *Loose Tooth*. Children love this game because they relate to losing teeth. Say the poem while having the children walk to the steady beat. You can add a drum beat to reinforce the steady pulse, but it isn't a requirement. Make sure the children walk in random paths around the room, not in a big circle like a mixing bowl.

> Loose Tooth, Loose Tooth, I have a Loose Tooth.
> A Wiggly Jiggly Loose Tooth a hangin' by a thread.
>
> I lost my Loose Tooth, my Wiggly Jiggly Loose Tooth,
> Put it 'neath my pillow and then I went to bed.
>
> Someone took by Loose Tooth, my Wiggly Jiggly Loose Tooth,
> Now I have a nickel and a hole in my head.

After the children are very comfortable walking to the steady beat of the poem, raise the difficulty level. Every time "loose tooth" is said in the poem, the children must turn and walk a different direction. Practice this several times, watching for the children to become more proficient at listening and changing movements at the correct point in the poem.

Next add in another requirement to the game. In addition to turning on "loose tooth," have children make their body wiggle and jiggle on the words "wiggly jiggly." Again, practice this part of the game, observing the children walk the steady beat, turn and go a different direction on "loose tooth" and wiggle and jiggle at the appropriate time. This doesn't seem particularly difficult, but moving, listening and doing all the different parts of the game require concentration, decision-making and self-discipline.

Finally, on "hole in my head," add in the last movement requirement. When they hear the words "hole in my head," have children tap hand on head rhythmically to the words.

This poem is reinforcement for discovering rhyming words and repeating words, and it is simply a charming activity for having a great time in class!

Shel Silverstein's book, *Where the Sidewalk Ends* is a treasure chest of poems.

Musical Games

"Partners and Pals"
"Oh Be Joyful"
 Line Dancing
"Head and Shoulders Baby"

Native American Name Game

word	movement	note value
Hiawatha	walk the beat	quarter note
Pretty Little Minnehaha	jog the words	eighth notes
Teepee	step bend step bend	half note
HOW (are you sir)	step bend bend bend	whole note

Tell a make-believe story about a little Native American Indian boy named Hiawatha who had a friend named Pretty Little Minnehaha who lived in a teepee. When they saw each other, they would say HOW (are you sir). After listening to the story, the children can practice the movements. Have the children stand and do the appropriate movement with each word. Tell the story again, this time with the children adding in the movements.

In today's world, the term "Native American" is accepted and considered "politically correct," although the term "Indian" is preferred in Oklahoma. In Oklahoma which is known as the Indian Nation, the term Indian is one of respect and a reference to its history as a state. Therefore a teacher can use the terms interchangeably with his or her class, and still be accurate.

Another variation on the game is to make large posters of each note. When you hold up the poster of the quarter note, the children walk the steady beat. When you hold up the poster of the eighth note, they jog the rhythm of "Pretty Little Minnehaha." Do the same with half note and whole note. This part of the game encourages observation skills.

Phyllis Weikert, an expert on movement and learning, believes that movement is important in language development with children. Her research indicated a link between a child's ability to clap a steady beat and the success in language learning. Through her research and publications Weikert has designed steps to use in helping children learn to move successfully. She recommends incorporating these strategies with teaching children movement:

- Say and do the movement

- Whisper and do the movement

- Think and do the movement

Thus, if you are teaching children the following movement pattern, step-step-bend-bend, you would instruct the children to do the movements as they say the words aloud. Then the children would progress to doing the movement pattern and whispering the words. Finally, they would "think" the words as they do the movement.

Additionally, Phyllis Wiekert's research suggests that both hands patting the knees at the same time in a steady beat is less difficult and therefore more successful that alternating hands on the knees. Thus, early experiences with steady beat should include activities in which the children pat their knees with both hands. As they become more proficient, begin with the alternating hands activity. Children will be keeping the beat as they pat right hand on right knee, left hand on left knee, keeping the pattern "right-left-right-left."

Marching can be a difficult movement for some children. Sometimes going through hand movement games prepares the child for greater success with the large motor skills required in marching. Such an idea will be reversed planning for many teachers. Often, even with very young children, a typical classroom scenario includes the teacher playing a music CD and directing the children to "march around the room to the music." By using the Weikert research, the children should be taught to keep a steady beat by tapping hands on knees before they are instructed to use the legs with marching. Then, when they do start to learn to march, having the child say and do, whisper and do, then think and do, sets the stage for more successful movement experiences.

Isn't it interesting that what is very simple for some children, like marching to a steady beat, presents a struggle for others. By teaching the "right" research driven method, a child can be successful in learning to move, and can be spared the frustration often resulting from "not knowing how" to move to the music.

Chapter 5

Creating

Children are naturally creative. They look at their world without limitations. A child thinks "what if" or "why not" rather than "you can't do that," when adults often apply to life restrictions such as "that would never work" or "nobody does it that way." As a result, guiding children into creative activities and encouraging creative expression should be natural, normal and vital components of the elementary curriculum. Such creative experiences can lead children into problem-solving approaches to thinking, establishing patterns of cognition that will prove beneficial to them throughout their lives.

Many adults believe that they are not creative. They will adamantly declare that they possess not even a hint of creativity in their whole being. Often an adult will jokingly describe the lack of creative ability with statements such as "I can't even draw stick figures." Some think to be creative means painting the Sistine chapel ceiling or composing the 9th symphony, which is true. However, creative thinking is also choosing a different blouse to wear with a different skirt than the one you usually pick, or deciding on a new recipe for using ground meat. It means looking at issues in different ways. Creative thinking means examining several different solutions to a problem.

Some writers on creativity believe that everyone is capable of being creative, although some individuals have had "blocks" placed on their thinking. Incidences in life happen that leave an individual feeling that he or she is not creative. When a teacher says not to color the chicken blue, the child's creative decision making is being blocked. Even though children are genuinely very creative, life experiences and statements from others tend to crush the creative spirit. Picasso said that he could paint like Rafael as a child, and then he spent the rest of his life learning how to paint like that again.

Today's world demands creative thinking in the work place. For our children to be able to contribute positively as adults, creative thinking is a necessity. Few aspects of life are "black and white" or have "one right answer." Do you buy a house or rent one or move into an apartment? Do you buy a new car or a used one, or do you lease a car? Do you sell your car and use mass transit? Do you replace the electric heater with gas? Do you refinance now or wait? How long should you wait until you refinance your home? All of these questions have many possible answers, all of which might be correct at a given time. The ability to problem solve and think with a "what if" slant to mental reasoning is a valuable and sought-after skill, and a required ability for living successfully in the world of the 21st century.

No longer can a child memorize enough facts to succeed in life. This child must be able to think creatively. Cancer cures will come from someone thinking creatively. Researchers must learn to examine situations from many different vantage points. The elementary teacher is training tomorrow's adults, the keepers of the flame, the voters who will decide on issues that will influence our world. These leaders of tomorrow must be provided tools to help them grow up and successfully take their place in society. They need to be given innumerable opportunities during their elementary schooling to think in creative ways.

Process in preference to Product
The following activities are designed to spur creative thinking skills in elementary students. One important key for teaching creative activities is to remember this:

> **PROCESS is more important than PRODUCT.**

The teacher should be more concerned that the children have many opportunities to think and act creatively, rather than being overly concerned with the resulting poem or painting or word choice. Often the product is not particularly memorable, and will probably not "live through a test of time." The more important aspect is that the child had the experience of being involved in the creative process.

Creative Thinking Levels

E. Paul Torrance, an early researcher in gifted education and creative thinking, developed a list or levels to move through in encouraging creative thinking.

1. *Fluent* — Letting the ideas flow
The first, or lowest, level of creative thinking

2. *Flexible* — Changing ideas, bending ideas
The second level of creative thinking

3. *Original* — Creating new ideas
The third level of creative thinking

4. *Elaborative* — Refining the ideas
Trying different approaches
The fourth level of creative thinking

5. *Evaluative* — Asking "what is correct" and "what could be improved"
Evaluating the work
The fifth and highest level of creative thinking

> Teaching Tip
> In using these Torrence steps or levels with children, start with words, a secure area.

One topic to which children will readily respond is breakfast cereals.

1. Have the children name different breakfast cereals, notating them on the board. (*Fluent*) The list will be long and varied because elementary students know many different brand names, thanks to the cereal aisle at the grocery store and Saturday morning cartoons.

   - One way for all the children to participate is to go down the line, or around the circle, having each child name a cereal. If choosing this plan, institute the "PASS" rule. If a child cannot think of a cereal to name, they say "Pass" and the game moves to the next child. This frees the children to think without pressure. The teacher should not comment on any children's contributions during this part of the activity. By saying, "Oh, what an interesting comment" to one child, the response from all the others tends to be, "I can't think of anything that good!" or "John is her favorite. Wonder why she likes him best?" Of course, these thoughts, foolish as they are, squeeze out the creative thinking, where the emphasis of the activity is really intended. By commenting on one child, the free flow of ideas has been limited for most of the others.

2. Next, arrange the words from the list into a rhyme or chant. In changing the ideas from a list of words on the board into a poem, a higher level of creativity is reached. (*Flexible*)

   - Decide on the rhythm of the words. "Grape Nuts" becomes two quarter notes or two eighth notes followed by a quarter rest, or a quarter rest followed by two eighth notes.

3. Clap the rhythm patterns, or clap the first line, snap the second line, pat the third and stamp the fourth line. (By choosing the word "stamp" rather than "stomp" to indicate making a sound with your foot, the teacher may eliminate some unwanted sounds from the class.) The list of words now is evolving into a rhythmic sound composition. It is no longer a list or words or a chant. It is a sound composition.
   (*Original*)

4. Transform the sound composition into an ABA or a rondo form. One could use body sounds for A and the words for B.

   - Add an introduction and a coda.
   - Use dynamics at some point in the composition.
   - Try different ideas, deciding which ones seem to work best.
     (*Elaborative*)

5. Tape the sound composition. Listen to it as a group. Have the children decide what was good about it and how it could be improved. (*Evaluative*)
   - Asking questions like "What did we do right?" or "What sounded especially good?," helps children point out the good parts.
   - Asking "How could we improve?" or "Where are our weaker parts?," still is phrased positively, but focuses on areas for improvement.

> It is very important to help children discover the positive.
> They tend to focus only on the problem spots, rather than recognize that many good points were achieved.

Compositional Formula

As an elementary music teacher, one of my goals was to help my students become composers. My nagging thought was, "Perhaps the next Aaron Copland is one of my students!" Yet, as a young teacher, achieving any sort of result from my creative attempts fell far short of my intentions. Once, in planning a creative lesson for a fourth grade class, the children were to be composers, using rhythm patterns to create compositions. "You can create anything," I remember telling them, emphasizing the word "ANYTHING."

By the end of the period, the children were chasing each other around the room as I stood in the middle of the class, wondering "What happened?" Now I know that setting limits seems to spur the creative experience. That fourth-grade lesson of many years ago was much too open-ended. The children needed more limits or restrictions for the process to be successful.

Through the years, I have experimented with creative activities for young students, and have developed a COMPOSITIONAL FORMULA. Using this formula will establish some requirements, set some limits, and will function as a tool for stimulating the creative experience.

The Compositional Formula

- Use a form
- Include dynamics in the composition
- Have an introduction
- End with a coda
- Add an ostinato

Although *the process is much more important than the product*, having the addition of an ostinato tends to hold the piece together.

An ostinato is an underlying repeating accompaniment. A boogie-woogie bass is a type of ostinato. A handclap pattern performed by several students can serve as an ostinato. Repeating phrases of sounds or words can be an ostinato. In a "cereal" composition, the words *snap, crackle, pop* followed by a finger snap can be performed over and over by a group of children as the rest of the composition is performed, somewhat "on top" of the ostinato, by the remainder of the children. The ostinato should be softer dynamically than the composition.

An introduction is something that goes before. It could be the ostinato performed a designated number of times before the composition starts. It could be four children tapping a drum eight beats, or a musical phrase sung or hummed. Whatever the composer decides is correct.

A coda is an ending. The word literally means "tail" in Italian. Again, the ostinato could be repeated several times, gradually getting softer (decrescendo   ). Or you could choose a loud crash on the gong to end the piece. Tell the children, "Remember, you are the composer. Whatever you choose is correct."

An example of a composition following the formula is:

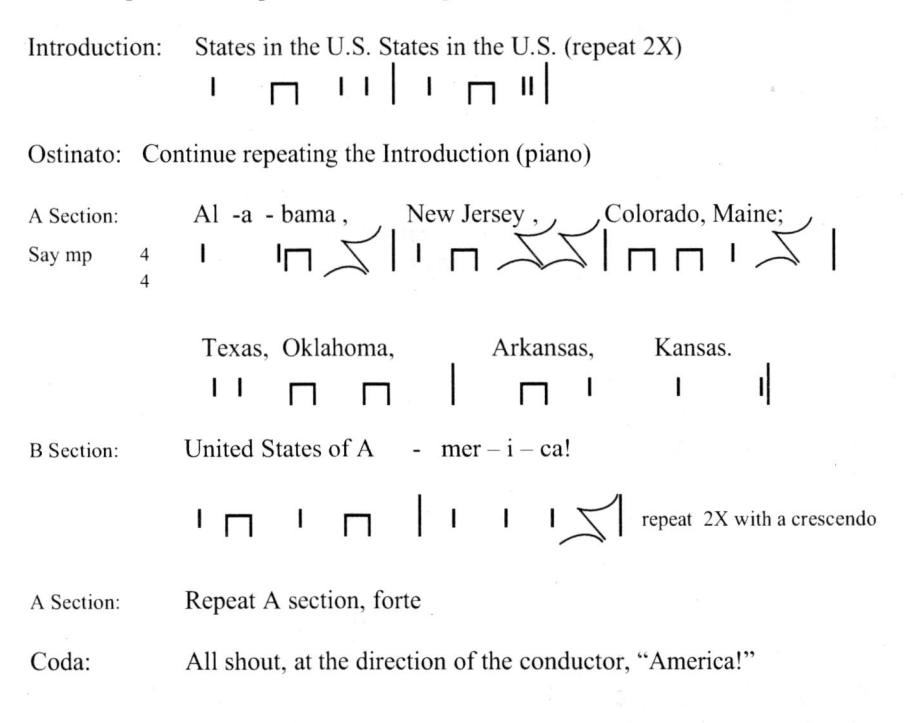

Introduction: States in the U.S. States in the U.S. (repeat 2X)

Ostinato: Continue repeating the Introduction (piano)

A Section: Al -a - bama ,   New Jersey ,   Colorado, Maine;
Say mp   4/4

Texas, Oklahoma,   Arkansas,   Kansas.

B Section: United States of A - mer – i – ca!

repeat 2X with a crescendo

A Section: Repeat A section, forte

Coda: All shout, at the direction of the conductor, "America!"

Simple activities for children using creative responses include:
(These can be done in cooperative learning groups or individually.)
- Explore three ways to play an instrument.
- Think of three ways to clap your hands.
- Find three different sound sources in our classroom that can be played.
- Walk to the door a different way.
- Find three ways to make a circle with your bodies.
- Make the first letter of your name with your body.

Telling the children, "There are 28 (whatever the number of children in the class) students in our class, and there can be 28 different compositions (or answers or examples), all correct," is an interesting thought for them. All of us can be right, and all different. These thought patterns can be further explored in discussing people who are different from us. How should people different from us be treated?

Exploring Body Sounds

Levels of body sounds for composition and accompaniment patterns can be another creative venture for the children. Make a four-line staff, where the top line is to be the "snap" sound, the second line the "clap" sound, and so forth. Notate the sound patterns by placing Xs on the lines, using the plan of four sounds in a grouping, or measure.

```
Snap__x_____x__x_____
Clap_____x_____x____x____x__
Pat _____x_____x___x_____
Stamp _____x_____x_____
```

The children can create many different patterns and perform them. They can sing a song while performing the patterns as they sing, which is quite demanding, rather like mental aerobics! They can number the different patterns, and then play number "!43" which is really numbers 1 and 4 and 3 played as a set.

Creating New Words to Familiar Tunes

Using TV theme songs, create new words to the tunes. These new "theme songs" will be used to gather children for different activities during the day. For example, the *Bat Man* theme could have the words:
        Math Time!
        Time to get our books and pencils, don't forget the paper either,
        Math Time!
        We are learning long division, We are getting good at reason,
        Math Time!

Children will sing the words as they get their books out and find the page in the book. By using music to "set the stage" for learning, the atmosphere in the classroom will be more inviting for engagement in math activities. Current brain research is showing us that music activates the brain for learning, and helps people retain information. What a wonderful combination! Math and Music!

Creating visual guides to music
To help students understand music more easily, a visual guide or listening map can be created. These maps help children listen with heightened awareness, thus understanding more about what they are hearing.

Section III

Helps for the Elementary Classroom

Infusing Music into the Curriculum

To transform learning from a "task to be done" into something fun and memorable, engage the children with music. Through lessons incorporating music, students learn to acquire knowledge which becomes more relevant and significant to them individually.

Music has the component of "play." We "play" an instrument to make it sound. Children learn through play, therefore music makes learning more like play in the mind of a child.

When the wise teacher draws on music to help teach other subjects, newness weaves into the material to be learned. The lesson isn't labor or drudgery, it is play! Music eases into the mind, helping bring freshness and originality to a learning task, and the brain makes connections in new ways.

Music rejuvenates the learning experience; it adds "umph" to the lesson; it supercharges the learning! What more do you want! Music is a key to open doors to teaching your children. Turn the pages to learn how to teach regular subjects more effectively!

Chapter 6

Using Children's Literature with Music

The incredible range of literature available to use with children is a rich storehouse for the elementary classroom teacher. Beautifully illustrated books of every conceivable topic line the shelves of most elementary school libraries. These books can become the catalysts opening pathways to learning experiences of great variety for the elementary child.

Exciting opportunities await the teacher who begins a lesson with a child's book. Part of the fun of using children's literature in the elementary class is watching how the learning evolves and grows. A lesson on creativity may expand into a social studies lesson. Another lesson geared to teaching multicultural awareness may develop into a session on musical compositions. A book read for sheer pleasure may awaken interest in a foreign language.

Elementary teachers use integrated curriculum, whole language, and interdisciplinary learning in their classes. Certainly they use children's literature in their classes. But often these approaches to learning are not extended to the arts. Using children's books for music teaching? Certainly, but with a warning label attached! Be sure to fasten your seat beats as the learning unfolds.

Relating to Reading

Music helps build the very basic foundation for learning to read. Children throughout the years have learned the alphabet by singing "The Alphabet Song" to the tune of "Twinkle Twinkle Little Star." Often they think "LMNO" or "LMNOP" is one word because they sing the song that way. By slowing down the singing and by having a child point to the alphabet as they sing, this misconception will be clarified, as the children realize that L is a separate letter, M is a separate letter, and so forth.

By having the words to songs sung in class displayed on a chart or on sentence strips in a holder, children are encouraged to read as they sing. We know from brain research that music helps children learn. Music helps their brains make connections, it is affective learning that helps them like to learn, and it helps them hear the rhythm of speech. It also helps them learn to sequence, to learn rhyming words, to understand syllabication, and to learn phonemic awareness. Words are made aurally, and a key to learning to read is to become aware of the sounds associated with reading.

Why would anyone try to teach reading without using music?

Catalyst to Creativity

The sounds suggested in children's books can come alive with music instruction. Sounds can accompany the story, turn into music, and even become compositions themselves as the children develop musically. For example, *Brown Bear, Brown Bear What Do You See?* and *Polar Bear, Polar Bear, What Do You Hear?* both by Bill Martin, Jr., are excellent books for having young children add sounds associated with words in the text. These books clearly use repetition and contrast to enable children to choose appropriate sounds. The children see the picture of an animal such as a lion and add a body sound or instrumental sound, creating a sound composition as they go through the book. As extensions of this lesson, the class can research information about bears such as their habitats and different types of bears as well as bears represented in art. A trip to the zoo with pictures drawn by the children of the animals could become the classes own book about Animal Animal, What Do You Hear?, or Where Do You Live? Or What Do You Eat?

FYI   The words to *Brown Bear, Brown Bear* can be sung to the tune of "Twinkle Twinkle Little Star."

After reading a book such as *Where the Wild Things Are* by Maurice Sendak, ask the children to think of places in the story for adding sounds. This story of Max, an adventurous boy sent to his room by his mother, suggests interesting sounds. After sharing the children's ideas, read the book again with class members making the sounds in appropriate places. Suggest next that the body sounds can transfer to percussion instruments and have the children select instruments to make the sounds. The tone block may become the sound of Max running, while glissandi on the xylophone may represent the sound of the ocean.

The instrument selection process in itself is a learning experience. Rather than selecting the instrument that makes the sound most like the character or event in the story, children pick their favorite instrument. Using this criterion, a child might pick a ratchet to make the sound of a snowflake. To guide the students in selecting appropriate instruments is a music lesson in itself, often one that requires persuasive teaching.

After choosing instruments, read the story again, this time with children adding the instrument sounds. Finally, tell the story using only sounds. Tape the sound story and listen to the composition as a class. Ask the questions "What did we do correctly?" and "Where could we make our composition better?" The evaluation process is a valuable part of this learning experience, requiring the children to use higher level thinking skills.

Sound Compositions
Creating sound compositions is another use of children's books. These compositions can range from the very simple, as in *Brown Bear, Brown Bear, What Do You See?* to more extended compositions. *The Jolly Postman*, by Janet and Allan Ahlberg, can lead to a delightful rondo. The book is written as a series of letters delivered by the postman to famous storybook characters. One class using this approach had the postman as the A Section. The postman's section had a recurring ostinato pattern that reminded the listener of a rickety bicycle wheel. The contrasting sections forming the rondo included the letter to the wicked witch as the B section, the letter from Jack to the giant as the C section, and Cinderella's letter as the D section.

The witch's letter was portrayed with cackly sounds made by a combination of metal and wooden percussion instruments. The giant's letter was composed of heavy walking sounds, as if made by the ponderous foot of the big fellow. Cinderella's letter had a magical, tinkly quality created by using metal bar and percussion sounds. The resulting rondo told the story, but in a different way.

Enhancing Reading
The following exercises use music to enhance reading and knowledge of literature. Children's books facilitate powerful learning and stimulate creative thinking skills. Try the example lesson below:

Getting Started
Cadillac, a book about riding in Granny's old pink vintage car, is full of rhythmic wording. The phrase "Shackalacka lacka," the sound the old car makes, repeats often in the book.
- Read the book to or with the class.
- Write the word "shackalacka" on the board or on a sentence strip.
- Have the children decide on a movement and or sound for the "shackalacka" sections, starting with body motions "looking like" the shackalacka phrase sounds.
- As the book is reread, children make the body sounds replacing the words on the shackalacka parts.

Expanding the Learning

1st. Arrange the children in small groups.

TEACHING TIP: Teacher can randomly assign children into groups by counting off "One, two, three, four, five… but a more effective grouping is to arrange the children according to their strengths. In each group, for example, include a child that is a leader, one that is more shy, one that is a helper, one that will be able to notate. This type of grouping, often called a cooperative learning grouping, is more likely to function well together.

2nd Have each group decide on a series of body motions and/or sounds that will fit with the rhythmic word "shackalacka." Give them 3 minutes to complete the task. Then share each group's results with the whole class, not taking more that 5 minutes. Read the first page of the book again, with all groups making the "Shackalacka" sounds together at the appropriate time.

Expanding the Learning AGAIN

3rd **Groups transfer their created body sounds to instruments.**

- Each member of the group will participate.
- Group must use at least one wooden sound and one metal sound.
- Sounds selected by the group must include a crescendo.

4th **Groups then share their decisions with the whole class.**
This sound collection can become the "A" section of a rondo

Rondo, a type of ABACA form. The returning "A" section occurs three or four times.

5th **Select words to be the "B", "C" and "D" sections.**
- Granny and the little girl riding in the car might be one section, Granny pulling into an intersection might be another, and the policeman writing a ticket could become the last section.
- You can simply read the words for each section, always returning to the "A" section with groups playing their instruments.
- Then, different children select instruments to make sounds for each section.
- The final result will be a sound composition in rondo form, performed by the class.
-

            A.   Shackalacka

-
        A. Shackalacka
        B. Granny and the little girl
        A. Repeat Shackalack
        C. Granny pulling into an intersection
        A. Repeat

The whole story of Granny and her old pink Cadillac, with the long fins and the gold flecks in the paint, can be told in sounds with no words. After the groups or individuals have decided on sounds and/or instruments for the sections, go through the book showing the pictures, having the groups perform their sounds with no words at the appropriate pictures. This telling of the story in sound is a forerunner to programmatic music, music intended to tell a story. (See chapter 3, page 34)

Expanding the learning AGAIN and AGAIN

Practicing reading skills is another advantage of the Cadillac lesson.
- **Using** sentence strips, write the words and phrases used for the composition.
- **Arrange** them in order in a holder, having the children follow the words as the Cadillac Rondo is performed.
- Then, let the children decide on other arrangements for the rondo. Perform.
- At another time, have the sentence strips out of order in the holder. Children must arrange them in the correct sequence.

Why Teach This Anyway?
Enrichment activities with reading offer enjoyment for the whole class as they explore many opportunities to read. The children will develop even more ideas. Movement could be added, words could be expanded into rhyming phrases; anything they want to create is possible. As the class begins to become comfortable with creating, the children will take this type of lesson to unknown destinations through their imaginative word play.

Activities with literature provide perfect special Friday-afternoon events. The classroom teacher can use longer periods of time engaging the children in creative experiences resulting reading enrichment and in musical compositions. Video and audio taping the class at work with these types of creative problem solving lessons embed evaluation and assessment in the process. Let the parents listen to the Cadillac composition during Back-to-School night. Explain to the parents how the children used creative problem solving to reach their decisions, how every child was involved, and how reading was emphasized along with the creative process.

Gardner's MI Theory
Howard Gardner's Theory of Multiple Intelligence can be included in the rationale for designing lessons such as Granny's *Cadillac*. Each of the intelligences is represented in this lesson.

Musical Intelligence	the rhythms of the words
Linguistic Intelligence	reading the sentence strips
Spatial Intelligence	creating movements
Intrapersonal Intelligence	Getting to express ideas
Interpersonal Intelligence	Working in the group
Mathematical Logical Intelligence	Ordering the sections
Artistic Intelligence	Creating a rhythmic composition

Some brain research indicates that such creative experiences utilize the brain in more "complete" thinking operations. Although the healthy brain never functions totally on one side or the other, the left hemisphere is brought into play with the sequencing, ordering, and reading, as the right hemisphere is used with the creative decisions. The emotions, housed in the cortex, are involved because it is fun to do this activity, and the area of the brain involved with emotions is also tied to motivation and memory. Children enjoying their work indicate great success for the learning environment and for the teacher.

Leading to Creative Writing
Students working in cooperative learning groups can capture in sounds the mood created in children's books. Remember to give specific directions to each group allowing maximum opportunity for a successful creative process.
- What is the emotion or mood suggested by the book?
- What sounds could suggest that mood?
- What instruments could suggest the mood?
- How should the instruments be played? (Loud or soft, in combination or singly, only one sound or repeated sounds?)

Letting each group take time to experiment with capturing a mood in sound will culminate in group products to be shared with the whole class. *Yonder*, by Tony Johnston, and *Home Place,* by Crescent Dragonwagon, are good books for creating a mood.

Extensions of this mood exploration await in creative writing assignments. When a teacher "primes" the students with previous creative experiences before a writing assignment, the resulting process and product can be much stronger. As a child, I remember being asked to write poetry or a story with no advanced preparation by the teacher. The frustration I felt many years ago is still part of my memory. When a child is properly prepared for a creative writing assignment, this frustration is replaced with anticipation.

Enhancing Musical Elements and Skills through Literature
With certain books, merely reading the story out loud lets the children experience the rhythms of the words. *Chicka Chicka Boom Boom*, by Bill Martin, Jr., and John Archambault, is a perfect book for helping children feel rhythm. Even the title suggests rhythms to the reader.

The captivating words and phrases in the book, centered around the ABCs, almost demand body movement from the listener. Several phrases repeat throughout the book. The same movement could be performed each time the repeated words are read, reinforcing the concept of same/different in music.

Several books by Peter Spier contain only pictures and can be used to introduce and augment learning about specific facets of sound and music. His books are quite detailed and could be used in small group settings or with individual learning experiences. *Crash!Bang!Boom!* can be a motivating addition to units on sounds and sound production. His *Noah's Ark* is an attractive picture book that can introduce the many folk songs about the story of Noah and the animals. Further study of music about animals might include listening to Saint-Saen's *Carnival of the Animals*.

Famous songs have inspired many authors of children's books. *Go Tell Aunt Rhody*, illustrated by Alibi, is a good book to read while learning about folk songs. Often in music class the children in 5th or 6th grade play this tune on recorder. Inviting these children to perform for your class is a way to give recognition to the music program, and to spread positive public relations in the school. Several books are available about *Old MacDonald*, and Paul Zelinski has published *The Wheels on the Bus* as a pop-up book. Simply having these books on display in the classroom can stimulate interest in reading for some children.

Cumulative books abound in children's literature, and through them children can practice sequencing and ordering, mental skills valued by educators. Additionally, musical score reading and following a conductor while playing percussion instruments are skills to be learned. *The Noisy Counting Book*, by Susan Schade and Jon Buller, is the story of a boy fishing at a pond who encounters many noisy insects and animals, all described cumulatively. Children can select percussion instruments, playing each time the insect or animal appears in the story. By taking the sound accompaniment concept a step further and designing a score for the instrument players, students can also practice music-reading skills. A student director conducting the piece completes the ensemble experience.

This non-traditional score is an example to use with *The Noisy Counting Book*:

Children select instruments to play for each picture. Then "read" the chart, adding the sounds as you do. One child will play the "frog" sound, another child will play two "duck" sounds, another will play three "bird" sounds, and the last child will play four "fish" sounds. The pictures could be rearrange, others could be added, letting the children play the chart again. This is both a reading exercise, and a creative activity.

Ben's Trumpet, by Isadora, is an imaginative story of a boy growing up in the 1930s. It introduces the instruments of a jazz ensemble. Reading the book also offers a historical perspective on life in a different era. This book could lead to learning about the life of Louis Armstrong, who grew up in racially segregated New Orleans about the same time period as is the book. Armstrong, known as Satchmo because he could fill his cheeks with air making them look like satchels when he played, became one of the world's best-loved performers. His playing trumpet and singing is heard on the song "What a Wonderful World" which can be used as an art experience for children.

Using the following list, assign children a number and instruct them to draw a picture that represents their sentence.
1. Draw a picture of trees with green leaves.
2. Draw a picture of red roses.
3. Draw a picture of flowers blooming.
4. Draw a picture of you and a friend.
5. Draw a picture of "thinking to yourself."
6. Draw a picture of a wonderful world.
7. Draw a picture of blue sky.
8. Draw a picture of white clouds.
9. Draw a picture of a bright sunny day.
10. Draw a picture of a dark night.
11. Draw a picture of you thinking about yourself.
12. Draw a picture of a wonderful world.
13. Draw a picture of the colors of the rainbow.
14. Draw a picture of the rainbow in the sky.
15. Draw a picture of faces of different types of people.
16. Draw a picture of different kinds of people walking past each other.
17. Draw a picture of friends shaking hands.
18. Draw a picture of friends saying, "How do you do."
19. Write the words, "I Love You," and decorate the paper around them.
20. Draw a picture of a baby crying.
21. Draw a picture of a child growing.
22. Draw a picture of a school.
23. Draw a picture of you thinking to yourself.
24. Draw a picture of a wonderful world.
25. Draw a picture of you thinking to yourself.
26. Draw a picture of a wonderful world.
27. Write the words "Oh, Yes," and decorate the paper around the words.

After the art work is completed, all children stand in a circle as the recording of

"Wonderful World" is played. At the appropriate time in the music, children hold up their pictures. Slides can be made of the pictures, and used as a slide show for back-to-school night, or the pictures can be scanned into a computer or digitally photographed for use with a multimedia production. This activity can be part of an assembly with several PowerPoints projecting at the same time. All the grade level classes can do the activity and have several pictures of the same phrase, so that three or four images project at the same time. Have the children standing on raisers, singing the song "What a Wonderful World," and you won't have a dry eye in the crowd. Parents and grandparents *love* this activity.

Learning Facilitators

We miss golden opportunities in the elementary classroom by not utilizing children's books for more than story time after lunch. Books facilitate powerful learning experiences for the children. They teach fluency and reading skills. They help children make connections between sounds of words and reading of words. Music and literacy compliment each other. Teaching with children's literature can stimulate creative thinking by transferring words to sounds and by capturing feelings through sounds. Musical learning about form and repetition and instrument recognition can also take place. Children can learn about other cultures and become better listeners as well. If you have not perused the children's section at a bookstore lately, a rich array of books is waiting to open the way for outstanding interdisciplinary learning.

Listing of Books for Use with Music Teaching

TITLES	Author Illustrator	Publisher	Notes
America the Beautiful	Illustrated by Neil Waldman	Atheneum, Macmillan Publishing Co.	Illustrations of the lyrics to the song.
Ben's Trumpet	Rachel Isadora	Greenwillow Books	Story of a boy growing up in the 20s.
Big Talk Poems for Four Voices	Paul Fleischman, Beppe Giacobbe illustrator	Candlewick Press	Poems to be read by four different children.
Brown Bear, Brown Bear, What Do You See?	Bill Martin, Jr. Eric Carle illustrator	Henry Holt and Co.	A much loved classic about animals and colors and much more!
By the Dawn's Early Light	Steven Kroll, illustrated by Dan Andreaseen	Scholastic Books	Story of the events leading to the writing of our National Anthem.
Cadillac	Charles Temple, Lynne N. Lockhart (Illustrator)	Putnam Publishing Group	A story about Granny's old pink vintage car, with wonderful rhythmic verses.
Chicka Chicka Boom Boom	Bill Martin, Jr. and John Archambault	Scholastic Books	Rhythmic Sounds and verse about the ABCs.
Christmas in the Big House, Christmas in the Quarters	Patricia C. McKissack and Fredrick L McKissack	Scholastic Books	Describes Christmas for the slaves and for the owners. Includes a cakewalk.
Classic Songs of America	Dan Fox	A Donna Martin Book	Illustrations from the Museum of American Folk Art.
Crash!Bang!Boom!	Peter Spier	Doubleday	Spier creates visualizations of sounds.
Crawdad, Doodlebugs and Greasy Greens	Doug Elliott	Native Ground Music	Songs, Stories and Lore celebrating the natural world.
Front Porch Old-Time Songs, Jokes and Stories	Wayne Erbsen	Native Ground Music	48 Great Sing-along favorites. Includes information about the music.
Get America Singing Again!	Project by MENC, forward by Pete Seeger	Hal Leonard	Collection of common song repertoire for singing.
Go Tell Aunt Rhody	Illustrated by Alibi	Simon & Schuster Children's Publishing	Pictures about the folk song of the grey goose.
Home Place	Crescent Dragonwagon, Jerry Pinkney, illustrator	Atheneum	A girl and her family discover an old home place, and find hints to the past.
I Hear American Singing Folk Songs for American Families (formerly	Kathleen Krull, illustrated by Allen Garns	Knopf	Collection of American folk songs for children. Beautiful illustrations and brief information

published as *Gonna Sing My Head Off!)*			about the songs. CD included.
I Wonder Why Stars Twinkle	Carole Stott	Kingfisher Books	Questions about Space.
Mirandy and Brother Wind	Patricia C. McKissack, illustrated by Jerry Pinkney	Alfred Knope, Publishers	Caldecott Winner, story includes a cakewalk.
Mole Music	David McPhail	Henry Holt and Co., New York	Story of a mole learning to play violin, and affecting others.
Musical Instruments	Gallimard Jeunesse and Claude Delafosse	Scholastic In.	Illustrated book of instruments and musical sounds.
My Favorite Things	Illustrated by James Warhola	Simon $ Schuster Gooks for Young Readers	Illustrations of song by Rodgers and Hammerstein from Sound of Music.
Noah's Ark	Illustrated by Peter Spier	Doubleday	Illustrations of the story of Noah's Ark.
Peter and the Wolf	Loriot, pictures by Jorg Muller	Alfred A. Knopf	A musical fairy tale by Sergei Prokofiev.
Philadelphia Chickens	Sandra Boynton	Workman Publishing, New York	Music with illustrations about an imaginary musical production, CD included.
Polar Bear, Polar Bear, What Do You Hear"	Bill Martin Jr, Eric Carle	Scholastic Books	Story of Animals and sounds.
Shaker Hears	Ann Turner	Harper Collins	Information concerning Shaker movement in America.
The Jolly Postman	Allan Ahlberg, Janet Ahlberg illustrator	Little, Brown Publishers	A set of notes, postcards and letters (included in the book) delivered to a cast of nursery rhyme characters.
The Noisy Counting Book	Susan Schade and Jon Buller	Random House	A cumulative book with sounds and counting.
The Star Spangled Banner	Illustrated by Peter Spier	Dell Picture Yearling	Illustrated version of the writing of our National Anthem.
The Wheels on the Bus	Paul Zelinsky	Dutton Children's Books	Adaptation of the traditional song with parts that move.
Traditional Songs of Singing Cultures: A World Sampler	Patricia Shehan Campbell, Sue Williamson, Pierre Perron	Warner Brothers Publications	Songs from around the world. Good information about music and culture. Teaching ideas and DC

			included.
Where the Wild Things Are	Maurice Sendak	Harper Collins Publishers	Caldecott winner, story of Max who takes a journey from his very own bedroom.
Yonder	Tony Johnston	Tony Johnston, Lloyd Bloom (Illustrator)	A plum tree shows the generations of a 19th century family.

Jennifer Heeren, a graduate in elementary education from Kansas State University, now an elementary teacher at Heritage Elementary School in Olathe, Kansas, bases her school year around children's literature. Jennifer was the winner of the Outstanding Master's Student award from the College of Education at K-State, and she shares this list with readers of *Face the Music*.

Listing of Books from Jennifer Heeren, Outstanding Elementary Teacher

Bunting, Eve	*Going Home*	Joanna Cotler Books (Harper Collins), 1996
Burleigh, Robert	*Hoops*	Silver Whistle (Harcourt Brace), 1997
Burns, Marilyn	*The Greedy Triangle*	Scholastic, 1994
Catrow, David	*We the Kids*	Scholastic, 2002
Cleary, Brian P.	*Dearly, nearly, Insincerely*	Carolrhoda Books, 2003
Clements, aAndres	*Double Trouble in Walla Walla*	The Millbrook Press, 1997
Deene, Ben	*First Encyclopedia of Seas and Oceans*	Scholastic, 2001
Fox, Mem	*Whoever You Are*	Harcourt Brace, 1997
Fox Mem	*Wilfried Gordon McDonald Partridge*	Kane/Miller, 1985
Gerstein, Mordicai	*The Man Who Walked Between the Towers*	Roaring Book, 2003
Gilman, Phoebe	*Something from Nothing*	Scholastic, 1992
Henkes, Kevin	*Chrysanthemum*	Greenwillow Books, 1991
Johnson, Stephen T.	*Alphabet City*	Viking Press, 1995
Joosse, Barbara M.	*I Love You the Purplest*	Chronicle Books, 1996
MacLachlan, Patrician	*All the Places to Love*	Harper Collins, 1999
Moss, Marissa	*Amelia's Notebook*	Tricycle Press, 1995
Nicholson, Sue	*Ocean Explorer*	Tangerine Press, 2001
Pattou, Edith	*Mrs. Spitzer's Garden*	Harcourt, 2001
Pinczes, Elinor J.	*A Remainder of One*	Scholastic, 1995
Rylant, Cynthia	*The Old Lady Who Named Things*	Harcourt Brace, 1996
Scieszka, Jon	*Math Curse*	Viking, 1995
Van Allsburg, Chris	*Two Bad Ants*	Houghton Mifflin, 1988

Chapter 7

Using Music with Science

Facts can be learned and retained amazingly well using rhythmic speech. The *School House Rock* television series proved this, and so does the long-running educational television icon, *Sesame Street*. Many people learned their ABC's to the tune of "Twinkle Twinkle Little Star." Making use of music to help students learn and retain information in the science curriculum also will produce good results. Even collegiate physics professors are learning this. Check out the website www.physicssongs.org. Dr. Walter Smith, Associate Professor of Physics at Haverford College maintains the website, and posts songs people have written about science. Smith uses folk tunes and familiar melodies ("Sweet Betsy from Pike," "Old Dan Tucker") and adds new words. He has found he is not alone, that many people enjoy using music to learn science. In using a web search engine, and typing in "Science Songs," over 6400 "hits" came up.

A few sites include: http://www.songsforteaching.com/sciencesongs.htm
Songs about measuring, growing seeds, the digestive system, the seasons, and numerous other cience topics are listed.
http://faculty.washington.edu/chudler/songs.html
Includes wonderful songs about the brain, to the tune of "Twinkle, Twinkle Little Star," The Dendrite Song to the tune of "Clementine," and other clever songs to help us learn about the brain.

Creating Science Songs
Of course, a class or group of children can write their own science songs. After a unit on a selected science topic, assign the students to groups and have them create songs using the information they learned during the unit. This song-writing exercise is an ideal outcomes based assessment of student knowledge as well.
- Select a science topic. (health, nutrition, the body, stars, the organs, functions of the organs, magnets, plants, measuring, and on and on)
- Select a tune from the following list: "Old MacDonald"
  "Bingo"
  "Row, Row Row Your Boat"
  "Down in the Valley"
  "Home on the Range"
  "99 Bottles of Beer on the Wall"
- Rewrite the words with lyrics describing the science topic
  1. List all the words you can think of about your topic
  2. Arrange these words to fit the rhythm of the tune you picked.
  3. Try to "make sense" with the words you picked
  4. You can try to rhyme your verses as well
  5. Perform for each other!

Creating Sound Compositions

When studying the body, children will retain more of the information by creating a sound composition using the terms learned. An example would be:

    Introduction: Our body, our body --- a smooth running machine

    Ostinato: Pump Blood Pump (clap)

    A section: Circulatory System
                    Heart pumps Veins carry
                    Arteries return

    B section: Heart   two chambers
                    Valves connect
                    Blood recirculates
                    (crescendo gradually during the B section)
    A section: repeat

    Coda: Keep it working! --- exercise!
               Keep it working! --- exercise!

Ideas for extending

A complete program could be produced about the body. Children could trace around each other on large sheets of butcher paper, coloring in facial features and drawing the shape of the organs inside their bodies. Large ziplock bags can contain the "intestines" which are really pieces of yarn cut to the actual length of a child's intestine. The heart could be shown in its actual size and location. All the systems of the body---circulatory, digestive, nervous and skeletal---could be demonstrated on these cutouts with overlays.

Let the children create rhythmic chants similar to the one above describing the various systems of the body and then present the information to parents or other grade levels in school. This musical presentation makes a delightful "Back to School Night" for parents, and it is effective instruction as well. The children will hold on to the information much longer than if a worksheet or notebook is the teaching method used.

Another bonus is that the activity also serves as an evaluation of the unit. As the children write the chants, the teacher can evaluate their understanding of terms and functions of the body.

One of the Barrenstein Bear books, *Junk Food*, would be helpful with younger children. The body systems are discussed by Brother and Sister Bear, and drawings of the body are included.

Bubble Games

A favorite activity for children of all ages is blowing bubbles. How many of us can remember getting a jar of bubbles at a birthday party and standing around blowing bubbles with our friends! Trying to blow the largest bubble before it burst, then watching it float to the ground, sometimes staying there for a second or two before it popped, was part of the fun. By combining the creative activity using words, poetry and music with science, a complete learning unit could be developed including spelling words, reading, art and design.

1. Have several bottles of bubbles, purchased from the discount store. Put them in your pockets and have children guess what you are carrying. Then show them the bubbles. Ask, "Are you sure its bubbles?" "How can we be sure?"

2. Of course, the answer is to open the jars and see if you can blow bubbles.

3. Let several children take turns blowing bubbles while the other class members observe the way the bubbles look and move.

4. Have the children give adjectives describing the bubbles which you list on the board. (*Fluent level* of creative thinking, see page   .) Let this activity go on for several minutes, until you have at least twenty terms on the board. At first the words will be simple, such as "round," "wet," "clear." Encourage the children to think of different ways to say "round," and different ways to describe they way the bubbles look and move. You will have quite a list generated by your students.

5. At this point, have several instruments displayed which might make bubble music. (Use lots of metal sounds, such as finger cymbals, triangles, glockenspiels and bells capable of producing sounds that relate to how the bubbles look and move.) (*Flexible, Original, Elaborative* levels of creative thinking, see page 64.)

6. Let several children make the music, randomly and quietly, remembering that the bubbles aren't always in sight. They seems to come in streams and float down to the floor, popping along the way. (*Original* and *Elaborative* levels of creative thinking.)

7. The other children are encouraged to write a poem about the bubbles, using words from the list if they want. The atmosphere in the room will be very quiet and soft. The children will be making "bubble music" and others writing, no voices allowed. (*Original* and *Elaborative* levels of creative thinking.)

8. The quality of the poetry is amazingly high. You can tape the music and have it playing during Parent/Teacher conferences, showing the poetry written by the children. (*Evaluative* level of creative thinking)

9. Include in the unit science exploration about the composition of bubbles.

Recipe for Bubbles

1 part	Use dishwashing liquid, Regular *Dawn* or *Joy*
10 parts	Water
.25 parts	Glycerine or White Karo Syrup (Optional)

Recipe for Super Bubbles

2 parts	Regular *Dawn* or *Joy*
4 parts	Glycerine
1 parts	White Karo Syrup

Body Bubbles

The body bubble, made with a hula-hoop and a child's small plastic wading pool, brings bubble making to a completely new level. Have a child stand in the wading pool, with feet in side the hula hoop. Then pull the hula hoop up over the child, making a very large body encasing bubble.

Type in "Bubble Making" on a search engine for the WWW and watch the hundreds of "hits" come up. Everybody seems to have a favorite bubble making recipe or an idea for a bubble maker.

Basic Bubbles I
½ cup Joy or Dawn dishwashing detergent
4 ½ cups water 3 to 4 tblsps. glycerin

Basic Bubbles II
1 cup dishwashing Joy or Dawn detergent
1 gallon water
1 tblsps. glycerin

Basic Bubbles III
1/4 cup liquid Joy or Dawn dishwashing detergent
3/4 cup water
1 ½ tablespoons light corn syrup

Bubble-blowing Devices

No matter what the shape of the bubble wand, the bubbles will be round. Another science experiment could be to examine different devices for wands and rate the effectiveness. A coat hanger bent into a circle works. Plastic cut-outs from milk jugs or heavy twine tied in a circle on a stick also make usable bubble blower wands.

Sound Waves

Sound is produced by vibrations and sound waves. The study of music, the aural art, is a logical place to study sound.

Many experiments can be completed by the students showing the relationship of length to vibration to sound. Rubber bands around a tissue box and the same length rubber band around a larger box show the difference in length and sound. Drinking straws cut in various lengths and blown across demonstrate the concept as well. Blowing across the mouth of pharmacy bottles holding different amounts of water also can be used. (Using pharmacy bottles with measurements on the sides helps children measure more accurately the amount of water.) A collection of *Snapple* ice-tea bottles can be arranged to play the scale, which must be created by the amount of water filling each one. Students selecting a variety of examples of length and sound experiments will prove their hypothesis that length affects pitch.

Palm Pipes

Another successful experience with the concept of length to pitch uses PVC pipe available at hardware and home stores. PVC pipe cut in different lengths makes different sounds when hit in the palm of the hand. The longer the pipe, the lower the sound.

using ½ inch PVC pipe:

Note	Length of ½" CPVC pipe for 180° water
F	23.60 cm
G	21.00 cm
A	18.75 cm
B flat	17.50 cm
C	15.80 cm
D	14.00 cm
E	12.50 cm
F	11.80 cm
G	10.50 cm
A	9.40 cm
B flat	9.20 cm
C	7.90 cm
D	7.00 cm
E	6.25 cm
F	5.90 cm

Taken from the following web site:
http://www.science.tamu.edu/CMSE/activities/PalmPipesChimesHints.doc

Students are able to play the following tunes, using the pipes.

"America"

f   f g e f g   a   a b flat a g f
My coun-try 'tis of thee, Sweet land of   li-ber-ty,

g f e f   c   c   c b flat   a
Of thee I sing. Land where my fath-er's   died,

b flat bflat bflat bflat a   g   a bflat a g f   a bflat c
Land   of   the   Pil - grim's pride, From   eve - - - - ry moun-tain-side,

d bflat   a g   f
let - -   free-dom ring.

"Yankee Doodle"

C C D E   C E   D   C C D E C B
Yan - kee Doo-dle Went to town, Rid- ing on a   pon-y

C   C   D E F E   D C   B   G A B C C
Stuck a fea - ther in his cap and   called   it "Mac- a -ro - ni,"

A B A G   A   B   C   G A   G F E G
Yan-kee Doo-dle Keep it   up, Yan - kee Doo - dle Dan-dy

A   B   A G A   B   C   A G   C   B D   C C
Mind   the mu - sic and   the step and with   the girls be han - dy.

A Good Website for Science and Music
By going to the Marco Polo Educational website, http://www.marcopolo-education.org, and clicking on the Arts Edge icon, many resources for teaching science and music can be found. Very helpful teacher resources include lesson plans, rubrics for evaluation of student learning, and extensions of the lessons

Body Music

Songs like "Head and Shoulders Knees and Toes" reinforce the parts of the body for children. Even the old warhorse "Hokey Pokey" teaches right hand, left hand, right foot, and so forth, again, reinforcing the parts of the body. The old song "Dem Bones, Dem Bones, Dem Dry Bones" tells musically a simplistic order of connection of the bones.

Animals, Science and Music

Animal crackers can become the catalyst for musical rhythmic compositions that start with facts about the various animals.

1. Students pick four different crackers from a sack. This activity works well with cooperative learning groups.

    - List facts about each of their animal crackers.

    - Books from the library, information from the internet, and resource materials could be used to gather these facts. For example, the list for camel might include words such as: humps
    can go long periods without water
    walks in sand
    carries heavy loads

2. Children then create a rhythmic composition incorporating the facts from the list about each of their four animals. Groups choose one animal chant as the "A" section of a Rondo, another animal chant as the "B" section, and the two other animal chants as "C" and "D." Performance of each group's Rondo (ABACADA) makes a wonderful closure to a unit on animals. (See page 24 in Chapter 2 on Form for additional information.)

Music about Animals

The study of animals should include listening opportunities as well. Many compositions have been created with the animal as theme.

Carnival of the Animals by Saint-Saens describes different animals in sounds. Ogden Nash wrote a poem about *Carnival of the Animals,* and an excellent video is available as well. The video, filmed at the San Diego Zoo, shows the animals as the Salt Lake City Children's Orchestra plays the composition.

Each section is short, which makes it very usable for children's attention spans. Playing a section without telling the animal makes a fun guessing game.

> Teaching Tip: Place the names of three animals on the board. Play a section of the music and have children decide on the correct animal. The music suggests the animal through the sounds, which makes this a good listening "work out" as well as study of animals.

14 Sections are included in the piece.

1. "Introduction and Royal March of the Lion"—the music portrays the king of the animals, the lion, as he walks along, as in a royal presentation. Listeners can also hear the lion's roar.

2. "Hens and Cocks"—the music sounds like chickens pecking and scratching along as they walk around. The rooster crowing is imitated by the music, and the listener can detect staccato notes.

3. "Wild Asses"— The music depicts these animals as fast running, "wild" creatures.

4. "Tortoises"--Saint-Saens shows his humor with this section. Offenbach's "can-can" melody, normally played fast, and often as accompaniment to dancers performing the very energetic dance, is used to portray the clumsy and slow turtle.

5. "The Elephant"—the music is a waltz, again a bit of humor about the large heavy animal.

6. "Kangaroos"—children love this section because it makes them think of the jumping Australian animal. They have great fun acting like kangaroos and jumping all around the floor.

7. "The Aquarium"—a very peaceful bit of music that reminds the listener of what it feels like to watch fish in an aquarium. Rather an interesting selection Saint-Saens includes in a "carnival" of animals!

8. "Personages with Long Ears"—the music is quite a contrast to the peaceful watery aquarium as it pictures in sound donkeys.

9. "The Cuckoo in the Forest"—the music portrays the bird in the trees which blurts out "cuckoo."

10. "The Aviary"—a musical picture of walking through the birds housed in an aviary of a zoo.

11. "Pianists"—again, Saint-Saens makes his listener ask, "What is he doing? Pianists as animals?

12. "Fossils"—a musical parady by Saint-Saens as he uses very familiar tunes including what we know as "Twinkle Twinkle Little Star" (French know it as "Ah vous dirais-je maman"), a bit of a Rossini aria from *The Barber of Seville* ("Una voce poco fa") and his own *Danse Macabre* where we hear skeletons dancing. He was telling us that these very familiar, perhaps overly familiar, melodies were like fossils in a museum. Through fame the tunes became dry little relics and more like artifacts than music.

13. "The Swan"—the music tells the story of a swan floating gracefully on the smooth pond.

14. "Finale"—the high spirited ending recaps clips from the various sections of the piece. Listeners must be extremely attentive because the musical hints of the lion, fossils, wild asses, hens and cocks, kangaroos, cuckoo, and pianists move very quickly in the music. Ending chords remind us of "Personages with Long Ears."

Swan Lake by Tchaikovsky is another animal theme musical composition. Several children's books discuss ballet and tell the story of this famous ballet. The story, similar to the ugly duckling theme, is a good one for children to know.

Flight of the Bumble Bee by Rimsky-Korsakov, is a musical tale of an insect. This work has been transcribed for many different musical groups ranging from trumpet solo to boogie-woogie to jazz quartets. The story of the bumble bee, which according to the size of the body and the smallness of the wings should not be able to fly, has reached "urban legend" status as well. Mathematicians and scientists have conducted numerous experiments on aerodynamics, mathematical studies about this insect. Using a search engine on the internet produces numerous "hits" with material about the topic. If it were a fixed wing airplane, it would not fly. The bee can fly because of the speed of its wing movements. This story has spawned many moral lessons about trying hard, working to achieve, and such.

"On the Trail" from *Grand Canyon Suite* by Ferde Groffe is about a donkey walking along the trail into the Grand Canyon. This programmatic composition tells the story in music of the donkey on the trail. The listening map helps students follow along with the music. Asking why the composer made a part that sounds like a music box is a good opportunity for students to think creatively. The correct answer is unknown, so everybody's idea is permitted. Possible answers might be:

- To symbolize water of the river at the bottom of the canyon seen at a great distance.
- To symbolize someone feeling "light headed" from the altitude of the canyon.
- To symbolize the sun sparkling on the canyon walls.

Additional games and activities appropriate in the study of animals include:

- List the animals which are athletic team mascots
  (Kansas State University Wildcats, Chicago Bears, LSU Tigers are a few.)

- List the animals used in cartoons or advertising
  (Bugs Bunny, Tony the Tiger, Winnie the Pooh, Tom and Jerry)

- Create a new animal with characteristics of two existing animals
  (Turbit….from rabbit and turkey)

- Study the habitats of different animals
  (A den or liar, nocturnal?)

- Learn the terms indicating a group of animals of one type
  (A gaggle of geese)

Weather and Music

Several composers have written music about storms. In the opera *William Tell* by Rossini, a storm is depicted by the music. (The "Lone Ranger" theme was taken from the "William Tell Overture.") Also, Ferde Grofe included a movement called "Cloud Burst" in his *Grand Canyon Suite*. Beethoven integrated a "Storm" in his Symphony No. 6 in F major (Pastorale). Vivaldi's *Four Seasons* includes a storm in the Presto from "Summer."

A great introduction to a study of weather would be to have the children make a "sound storm." Begin with one or two students snapping their fingers, and gradually adding in all the students snapping their fingers. This sounds like rain falling. Then have a few students change from finer snapping to patting their hands on their thighs. Continue to add in more and more students patting their hands until all are making the sound of rain falling hard, like the sound of a storm. Then gradually have the students change from the hand patting to snapping fingers, making the sound of rain drops. Finally, have more students stop making sounds until only a few are snapping fingers, making the sound of the rain beginning to stop.

Intersperse listening to these musical compositions with the scientific study of weather. Asking students to answer how the composers made the music sound like weather would include discussions of instrumentation and dynamics.

A New Scientific Experiment:

Wise teachers employ a variety of methods to enhance student learning, and using music to improve the study of science will open doors to understanding for students. Plus, engaging the mind in new ways is really the perfect scientific experiment. Try this theorem in your class, and watch the transformation begin.

> Music helps students learn about science in extended ways. The mind is opened to learning about science in different ways through the use of music.

Perhaps keep a log of which students seem more attentive when relating the study of science to some aspect of music, as mentioned in the activities suggested in Chapter 7 Notate the interesting comments from students, and the extended learning about scientific methods that are evidenced in your classroom. Learning science with music entwined would be an ideal approach for many children, and you may be surprised at which students seem to progress more quickly with this approach. Some students who never seem interested in the sciences will be drawn to the topic when using music as the learning vehicle. Enjoy this scientific experiment with your students.

Chapter 8

Using Music to Enhance Math Learning

Much of music is mathematical. The notes in music are divisions of a whole and have certain numbers of beats. Measures in music are intended to include the correct number of beats according to the meter signature. Meter is grouping of beats or sets of beats. The staff has five lines and four spaces. Melody in music is often patterns of sound. Harmony is two or more tones sounding together. Thus, using music to enhance math in the elementary school is a logical combination.

Reinforcing Math Skills
Counting

"Ten Little Indians"
"This Old Man"
"One, Two Tie My Shoe"

Many children's songs include counting. As children sing these songs, they are reinforcing their understanding of counting, and they are learning about their American heritage through music.

"Ten Little Indians"
One little, two little, three little Indians,
Four little, Five little, Six little Indians,
Seven little, eight little, nine little Indians,
Ten little Indian boys.

Of course, the song can be sung with "ten little Indian girls" as well. Have girls stand on the "girl verse" and boys stand when singing the "boy verse" at the appropriate point in the song, giving the children a visual picture of one, two, three and so forth. Do the song again, substituting the word "children" at the end. Then use a mix of boys and girls with the standing game. Have the words on a chart so the children see the words, learning the written word that corresponds to the number. At one point, this song would have been considered politically incorrect to use in a classroom. However, in Oklahoma, the term "Indian" is preferred to the word "Native American" because Oklahoma is the Indian Nation, and it is considered a term of great respect. Plus, this song is part of the body of American folk song, and should be taught to the children.

"This Old Man, He Played One"
This old man, he played one,
He played knick knack on my thumb,
With a knick knack paddeywhack, give a dog a bone,
This old man came rolling home

Each verse of the song adds a number, with new rhyming words, always ending with the "knick knack paddeywhack" verse. Other verses can use the following words, although many versions exist because folk music comes from an aural tradition.

Two-shoe
Three-knee
Four-door
Five-jive
Six-sticks
Seven-heaven
Eight-bate
Nine-shine
Ten-hen

Singing includes holding the correct number of fingers up for each verse, and making up a hand-jive part for the last two lines. Some snap fingers on the "knick knack," patting the knees with alternating hands on "paddeywhack," and doing of motion of tossing a bone over your shoulder for the "give a...." part. Then make a rolling motion with both hands on "rolling home."

"One Two Tie My Shoe"
One, two tie my shoe,
Three, four, shut the door,
Five, six, pick up sticks,
Seven, eight, lay them straight
Nine, ten, a big fat hen.

Saying the chant, holding up the correct number of fingers is a great time-filler to use before lining up for lunch or recess. Saying the chant in your head, silently, is an easy way to get children to walk down the hall quietly. They continue to hold up the appropriate fingers as they sing silently.

The original version said "buckle my shoe." Older children can be asked what that meant, and why did someone substitute the words "tie my shoe?" These discussions require higher level thinking skills. Students in upper grades can be assigned to small groups to create a more modern version of the chant. They might choose to substitute more current wording for the chant, creating a 2005 rhyme. They could use higher numbers or exponents or multiplication to make this activity more challenging, both mathematically and linguistically.

The Discovery Toys company CD, *Sounds Like Fun*, includes a song "Count to Ten" that reinforces the skill of counting by tens. Laurie Curtis, an outstanding kindergarten teacher used this song on the 10th day of each month, both reinforcing the number 10 and the concept of counting by tens. Singing the song with the children, when they reached the point in the lyrics about the number 100, they would all jump up. By the end of the school year, after using the song each month, Curtis said that all her children could count by 10s.

Subtraction

"Ten in the Bed"
"Five Little Monkeys"
"Allison's Camel has Ten Humps"
"Four Little Speckled Frogs"

"Ten in the Bed," "Five Little Monkeys," "Allison's Camel," and "Four Little Speckled Frogs" all deal with subtraction. In "Ten in the Bed," the little one says "roll over," and one falls out, leaving nine.

"Ten in the Bed"
There were ten in the bed
And the little one said "Roll over, roll over,"
And they all rolled over and one fell out.

The song continues until the little one is alone in the bed with lots of room, and comfortably sings "good night." Children, sitting in a circle, holding cards with a number on each become part of the math game. When the song sings "there were nine…" the child holding the 9 card stands up.

Nursery rhymes, jump rope chants, and folk tales include counting and subtraction, and again reinforce these numerical concepts for children.

"Five Little Monkeys"
Five Little Monkeys jumping on the bed
One fell off and bumped his head
Called for the doctor, the doctor said,
"No little monkeys jumping on the bed!"

The chant can be continued subtracting with each repetition. Four Little Monkeys, Three, and so forth until "No little monkeys" is what is left. Hand puppets, paper sack puppets, finger puppets can be made or purchased commercially to use with this chant.

"Allison's Camel"
Allison's camel has 10 humps,
Allison's camel has 10 humps,
Allison's camel has 10 humps,
So go, Allison, go! Boom Boom Boom

When the number is sung in "Allison's Camel," children hold up the correct number of fingers. So in the first verse, all ten fingers are held. On the words, "Go, Allison, Go" the punch their hands rhythmically out in front of them three times, once on each word. On the "boom boom boom" part, the children bump hips with the child on each side in the circle, once on each boom. This takes some teaching of self-control to keep them from bumping too rambunctiously and sending the neighbor child to the floor. If the class can't handle the bumping at first, just have them put their hands on their hips and shift their hips to the right and left. On each verse, subtract one "hump," so that the song is sung with nine, eight, and so forth, with children holding up the correct number of fingers with each verse. The song ends with zero, "Allison's camel has NO humps." Children make a zero with their fingers on this last verse, which ends with the spoken words, "because Allison's camel is a horse!" This song is a favorite of the lower grades, and they think the ending is a hysterically funny joke.

"Four Little Speckled Frogs"
Four little speckled frogs, sitting on a speckled log
Eating a most delicious fly

—yum, yum, yum,

One jumped into the pool
Where it was nice and cool
Then there were three little speckled frogs

Children sing this song, motioning with their hand in a circular pattern on their tummys, on the yum parts. Again, after the frog jumps into the water, children must subtract, and find the number of frogs left on the log.

Addition

"One Elephant'
One elephant, went out to play,
Out on a spider's web one day,
He had such enormous fun,
He called for another elephant to come.

In singing "One Elephant," the children can walk around like elephants, swinging their trunks. After they are secure with the song, have only one child do the walk part, until the words, "call for another." The first child picks a second child to come play, thus adding another "elephant." They now sing, "Two elephants went out to play." The game should add all the children. For practice with addition, the first "elephant" adds two more, so how many will we need? Add five more, and decide on the correct number of "elephants" who should be out walking.

Many CDs are available with helps for learning a variety of subjects, including math. Hap Palmer has written scores of creative, useful CDs that help children learn. As stated on his website, "Hap Palmer is an innovator in the use of music and movement to teach skills and encourage the use of imagination." Anyone who has used his recordings agrees! Among his award winning musical recordings which teach math are:

Two Little Sounds: Fun with Phonics and Numbers	2004
Singing Multiplication Tables	1971
Math Readiness	1972

Predicting

"Three Little Pigs" is the much loved children's story about the pigs who build their houses, only one of which withstands the "huffing and puffing" of the bad wolf. The story teaching many lessons, including work ethic and making wise decisions, but it can also be used to practice prediction. What happens to the first house thrown up very quickly by the first pig when some big wind blows on it? How many houses are left standing? Where are the other two pigs going? Good discussions with the children bring a better understanding of the three original houses, with suggestions as to why only one was left standing.

Patterns
Music has repeating patterns which children can discover both aurally and visually. Rhythm patterns are often repeated within a song, as are melodic patterns. When looking at music, help the children discover these repeating patterns.o

Musical Notation
The notational system for music is based on a numerical structure, so it is filled with opportunities for mathematical/musical learning. The traditional notation used for writing music includes numerical values.

In 4/4 meter signature, the following number of beats is given to each note:

Whole note	4 beats
Half note	2 beats
Quarter note	1 beat
Eighth note	½ beat
Sixteenth note	¼ beat

The half note is one half of a whole note, thus the name "half note." All the notes listed above have the same system. The quarter is one fourth of a whole, the eighth is one eighth of a whole, and so forth.

Many teachers draw pie charts showing the relationship of the different notes to the whole, and have children try to learn the fractions of the whole. Most children struggle with this concept. Expecting children in the first or second grades to understand fractions, such as a quarter note represents one fourth of a whole note is not a good plan. Piaget's research gives us the answer.

The work by Piaget places children in developmental stages or levels, and they learn in relation to certain characteristics within each level according to his research findings.

Piaget's Stages of Cognitive Development

Stage	Years	Cognitive Development
Sensorimotor	0-2 years	motor-action learning
Preoperational	3-7 years	intuitive learning
Concrete Operational	8-11 years	logical with concrete experiences
Formal Operations	12-15 years	abstract thinking

According to Piaget, the preoperational child cannot understand such concepts as fractions of the whole. Of course, these are generalizations to the children's learning abilities, and there are "exceptions to the rule." Generally, avoid teaching fractions before the fourth grade.

FYI:
(Before I had children, I was always a bit skeptical of Piaget's work, but the afternoon I gave my young child a cookie, all that changed! The cookie broke in half, but my son did not want to accept the two halves. He insisted on getting a *whole cookie*, even though the two halves really were a *whole cookie*. My son, age 3 at the time, was not cognitively developmentally able to understand that two halves make a whole. In his mind, the two halves were less that a whole. At that moment, Piaget's stages which I had learned in education courses became more real to me. I saw his research being demonstrated in the actions of my own pre-school child. I now believe!)

Teaching Notes through Movement

A better plan for teaching note names would involve body movement.
- Have large sketches of the notes on poster boards.
- Have the children move according to the note which is being displayed on the easel or on the board. Change the poster after you see that the children are doing the correct movement.
- Let one child play a steady beat on a drum.
- For a whole note, children will step on beat one and bend their knees three times to indicate the four-beat value of the whole note.
- For the half note, they step and bend, showing the two-beat value.
- The quarter note, often called the walking note, is shown by one step for each beat.
- The eighth note is shown by jogging.

Clapping Note Value Game

Children can also say and clap the note names as part of the learning of the number of beats or counts for each note. Use the following game:

Say as you	Do
Whole note, three, four	Clap once and keep hands clasped, moving them downward a few inches on beats two, three and four
Half note	Clap and clasp on beat two
Quarter (said to the beat.)	Clap once on each quarter note, thus the clap goes with the "quar" syllable of the word quarter.
Eighth Note or Two Eighths	Clapping on each word, thus, two claps per beat.

This game works well, except for the quarter note plan. The word "quarter" has two syllables and the quarter note only gets one beat. That can be confusing for some children. Some teachers say "quart" for the quarter note to avoid the misunderstanding.

Reading Notation
Children can read lines of notation using this game. The following line of notation would be read:

Quarter   Two eighths   Half-note   Quarter   Quarter   Two eighths Quarter

Then, they can write the rhythms mathematically. The line would be written:
$$1 + \tfrac{1}{2} + \tfrac{1}{2} + 2 \;=\; 4 \;+\; (1 + 1 + \tfrac{1}{2} + \tfrac{1}{2} + 1) = 8$$

Rhythm patterns can be represented using Cuisenaire rods. The longest rod would be representing the whole note, the half note would be presented as a rod half as long as the whole note rod, the quarter note would be ¼ of the length of the longest rod, and so forth.

Math problems could be stated in musical notation.
- The end result is 9 ½. Represent this total using musical notation.

- Combining notes from the note packet, make four measures, with each measure equaling 5 beats.

- Think of words to represent meter in 3s (basketball, blooming rose, tennis team)

- Think of words to represent meter in 4s (K-State football, Burger King fries, cappuccino)

- Bounce a ball to show meter in 2s, 3s or 4s. Get a partner and work out a game showing all three meters as you bounce the ball to each other.

In the chapter on Creating, an activity using TV theme songs is discussed. Children create new words to the famous TV tunes. One example used the *Bat Man* theme with math words:
        Math Time!
        Time to get our books and pencils, don't forget the paper either,
        Math Time!
        We are learning long division, We are getting good at reason,
        Math Time!

Children will sing the words as they get their books out and find the page in the book. By using music to "set the stage" for learning, the atmosphere in the classroom will be more inviting for engagement in math activities. Current brain research is showing us that music activates the brain for learning, and helps people retain information. What a wonderful combination! Math and Music!

Chapter 9

Music to Understand our World

The goals and objectives for most elementary schools include understanding other cultures as well as our own American culture. Most national standards in elementary education, as part of their goals or outcome statements, include global understanding or knowledge of other cultures. The arts provide perfect means for exploring other peoples and the history of our own nation. What remains from any lost civilization is the art, and no culture or group of people has ever existed that did not have music.

Multiculturalism is a familiar concept for teachers. Colleges structure courses devoted to teaching about people from backgrounds different from our own, and school districts sponsor workshops and in-services for teachers on the topic. Americans are proud of their diverse roots. Cities such as Chicago are famous for their neighborhood festivals celebrating the different nationalities represented by the citizenry.

It almost seems that teaching about multiculturalism is more successful than teaching about our own native culture and country, America. Watching *The Tonight Show*, when Jay Leno does his "Jaywalking" episodes glaringly indicates how little the average person on the street knows about American history.

In order for children to truly learn about our world, they need to know about our own country and culture in addition to knowing about countries and cultures around the world. We in education must be on a dual track, making sure we teach our students about America, our history, our heroes, our culture, along with exposing these youngsters to the people of the world.

Our world is shrinking, due in part to ready access to media and technology. Every night on the news we watch people from all over the world. Even wars fought on other continents are televised for instant viewing. We type in a web address and instantly are connected to sites filled with information about other nations, other cultures, world religions, music of the world….just any imaginable international topic is available.

Consequently, the big wide world is "out there" and all those cultures have music. Yet for many teachers, especially those trained more than a decade ago with no course work on the topic of world music, teaching multicultural music remains a difficulty. Fear of teaching this music improperly, mispronouncing the words, or abusing ethnic traditions is all the excuse some need to avoid including multicultural art examples altogether.

Music including folk dance, ethnic instruments, and cultural uses are included in all the series books available for use in our schools. Record and music stores have large inventories of folk music. Music from other nationalities or cultures is readily available through school supply catalogues and companies. (See appendix, page   ) As with most new things, getting started is the hardest part.

Multicultural Student Populations
Starting with the background of children in the class is a logical beginning. Often family members are more than willing to visit the class to share music from their native country. Amazing diversity will be represented by any one classroom of students, and encouraging them to discover their cultural origins can be an extraordinarily meaningful family project.

One music teacher, Janet Armstead, sends a note home at the beginning of the year asking if any families represent other cultures. She has never been disappointed with the results from her survey. By starting with the cultures of the children in class, and then progressing to other more distant countries and cultures, seems less daunting and more manageable for both teacher and pupils.

Multicultural Awareness through Children's Literature and Music
A wonderful book for expanding the awareness of the African American culture is *Talking Eggs*, by Robert D. San Souci with pictures by Jerry Pinkney. This fascinating folk tale of the rural South tells the story of Blanche, a Black child with a "spirit of do-right" and her sister Rose who is selfish and mean. This book would provide the libretto for an opera performed by an elementary class. This opera performance could be sung by improvisation in only one class period, or it could be composed and presented in "real opera" format for the school or parents. Set design, costuming, lighting, and staging would be hands-on learning. The performers could be children in the class or puppets created by class members. A memorable operatic event taking a variety of forms could be the result---all from reading one book in class.

Several books are available for sharing the Native American culture. *Hiawatha*, by Henry Wadsworth Longfellow with pictures by Susan Jeffers, is an artfully illustrated section from the original poem. *The Legend of the Indian Paintbrush*, retold and illustrated by Tomie DePaola, can serve as a wonderful introduction to a listening experience with Native American Music. Several recordings of authentic Native American music available include the following: *Songs Chants and Flute Music of the American Indian*, *Tribal Songs of the American Indian*, and *Authentic Music of the American Indian*, all by various artists and all available through *Amazon.com*.

At the Crossroads, another Isadora book, is an energetic tale of South African children waiting for their dads to come home from working in the mines. At one point in the story, the children make up a lively musical piece using some instruments they have. The book, while describing another culture, could also be a starting point for a composition.

Several books about Latino/Hispanic culture could be used in the music curriculum. *New Shoes for Silvia*, by Jonhanna Hurwitz, includes some Spanish words and would be a lead-in to the rhythmic chant "New Shoes."

>New shoes new shoes
>Red and pink and blue shoes
>Which ones would you choose,
>If you could buy?

The story could be told in verse that the children create, interspersed with the poem "New Shoes." The sounds of shoes walking could be played on found sounds or on percussion instruments borrowed from the music room.

The poem should also be learned in Spanish. To give children the ability to communicate in a language other than their own culture's is a gift. In teaching this creative musical lesson about shoes, the Spanish text could be interspersed with the English text for the rhythmic composition.

>Zapatos nuevos, Zapatos nuevos,
> Zapatos roho, y rosa, y azur
>Cual escogerias tu
>?Si lo pudieras comprar?

The Tamrind Puppy and Other Poems, by Charlotte Pomerantz, is a wonderful collection that incorporates Spanish text with English text in a creative manner.

Now to our American Story…..

Patriotic Music
Patriotic music of our country includes songs and compositions that every child living in America should know. Never should a teacher feel awkward about teaching a child from another culture songs about America. Many immigrants from other countries tell stories of how they go home and sing American songs and folksongs to help their family learn about their new home. This practice doesn't mean that you are asking the child to denounce their own heritage, but rather to add information about their "host" country. Many of these children will go on to become American citizens or decide to become dual citizens. Knowledge of American music helps them adjust. It is a gift, not an offensive act.

In the past music teachers always taught American music and American folk songs as part of their music curriculum. Some teachers had sing-alongs in the gym with all the children in the school singing songs of our country together. This body of literature, once standard fare, dropped from popularity during the Vietnam War. With political unrest and demonstrations raging against our country, the 1960s were a time when patriotism was under scrutiny, and some teachers began to ignore the valuable heritage of American patriotic music.

Folk Music
Dr. Marilyn Ward, in her doctoral dissertation from the University of Florida in 2004, surveyed each state as to inclusion of folk music in the curriculum. The state most likely to teach folk music is Nebraska, with Kansas a close second, and the state most likely not to teach folk music is California. She discovered through her research the disturbing information that Americans no longer know our own folk music. How sad that we in education are turning our backs to this vital and important part of our cultural heritage.

Teaching music of our country is an aural key to our past, and a way to experience history in a "now" time frame. Songs sung today can be the same as songs sung 100 years ago. History becomes more "living" when approached through music.

Successful Strategies for Teaching America's Music

The National Anthem
Reading the books, *The Star-Spangled Banner*, by Peter Spier, *The Dawn's Early Light*, by Steven Kroll, or *America the Beautiful*, by Katherine Lee Bates with illustrations by Neil Waldman, can provide children a clearer understanding of the texts of the songs.

The story of the writing of the "Star-Spangled Banner" by Francis Scott Key is not only a story of patriotism, but one of friendship, too. Key's friend Dr. Bean, a dedicated physician helping both the Americans and the British during the War of 1812, had been captured by the British. Francis Scott Key, a lawyer determined to gain his friend's freedom, went to the British battle ship anchored in the Baltimore bay where Bean was being held, to demand his release. During the time Key boarded the British boat to plead his friend's case, the battle at Fort McHenry had begun, thus forcing him to remain on board the ship. This long night he spent watching the raging battle from the deck of the boat, and the moving experience led him to write the words of our national anthem.

All Americans and students studying in American schools need to be familiar with the words to the National Anthem, and should know the story behind the song. Out of respect, students should stand and sing the song, just as Americans would stand for another countries' National songs.

MENC, the national music educators organization, has a project to encourage all teachers to "Get American Singing Again" our national anthem. A 2005 press release provides the following information:

MENC: The National Association for Music Education to Launch Project to Restore America's Voice in March 2005

RESTON, VA (May 21, 2004)– MENC: The National Association for Music Education is pleased to announce Mrs. Laura Bush, First Lady of the United States, as the Honorary Chair of The National Anthem Project: Restoring America's Voice.

The association is launching the National Anthem Project to renew national awareness of American traditions, promote the significance of "The Star Spangled Banner," and re-teach America to sing the National Anthem through a three-year national consumer education campaign.

"I am pleased to serve as the Honorary Chair for this important cause dedicated to preserving and promoting awareness about our country's National Anthem. I applaud the National Association for Music Education for their commitment to one of America's greatest traditions," said Mrs. Bush.

The National Anthem Project is expected to kick off in March 2005 and will include major singing celebrations throughout the country–at schools, professional sporting events and other local venues. The program to get America singing is planned to culminate with a record-setting performance of the National Anthem–hosted in Washington, DC in 2006 with simulcasts of local performances from "National Anthem Cities" across the country. For more information about the National Anthem Project: Restoring America's Voice, visit www.thenationalanthemproject.org.

More Patriotic Music
"When Johnny Comes Marching Home," a Civil War song, is the tune used as a theme and variation in *American Salute*, an 20TH Century instrumental composition by Martin Gould.   The theme, "When Johnny Comes Marching Home" is heard first by the -----------, playing softly. The theme is played….more times, with each variation changing to keep the listener's attention.   Theme and variation can be effectively taught by using Coke cans or potato chips (See page 25, Chapter 2.)

"Yankee Doodle" is the theme of several children's books which can be read as a class. The song was actually sung by the British soldiers to make fun of the colonist rebels who were fighting during the War of Independence. These "rag-tag" fighters were in stark contrast to the British regiments who wore their bright red uniforms, and were skilled in fighting in rows. (The movie *Patriot* gives a good visual picture of the difference between the British fighting forces and the American colonists striving for independence.)The American rebels wore whatever they could find, and fought in non-traditional ways, from behind trees or hiding however to ambush the more highly trained British army. What was intended as a musical insult became a favorite song of the American rebels, often sung to taunt the British!

America, the Beautiful, the words originally written by Katherine Lee Bates as a poem, has become a treasured patriotic song. Ms. Bates was traveling from her home in Massachusetts, where she taught at Wellesley College, to teach a summer course at Colorado College. She traveled by train, going first to Chicago to attend the Columbian Exposition in 1893, then on to Colorado. Throughout the trip, she experienced the different parts of the country, and became aware of the beauty and variety of the land and its people. When in Colorado, she took a trip up to Pikes Peak, and later wrote:

> "One day some of the other teachers and I decided to go on a trip to 14,000-foot Pikes Peak. We hired a prairie wagon. Near the top we had to leave the wagon and go the rest of the way on mules. I was very tired. But when I saw the view, I felt great joy. All the wonder of America seemed displayed there, with the sea-like expanse."

Katharine Lee Bates wrote the original version of "America the Beautiful" in 1893 as a poem. She wrote the 2nd version in 1904. Her final version was written in 1913. Many people started putting the poem to music so it could be sung. One tune used was "Auld Lang Syne" before the tune we now recognize, "Materna," composed by Samuel A. Ward in 1882, became the accepted version. The tune we recognize was composed nearly a decade before the poem was written.

Katharine Lee Bates never realized or wanted any royalties from her work, but she retained the copywrite to maintain the integrity of her written verses. In essence, she gave the song to the American people.

Books include:
America the Beautiful: A Pop-up Book
by Katherine Lee Bates, Robert Sabuda (Illustrator)

America the Beautiful by Katharine Lee Bates, Chris Gall (illustrator)

America the Beautiful by Lynn Sherr This book gives a history of Katherine Lee Bate's life, and what led her to write the poem we know and love.

Elementary school libraries will be filled with books about "America the Beautiful" as well as other books about patriotic songs.

Slave Songs
The years of slavery in the early centuries of the United States can be documented by a study of spirituals. The incredibly beautiful genre of folk music given us by the slaves is a great life's lesson. Slavery, a dark and horrific part of our American history, produced the beautiful art form of Negro spirituals. Are we sorry that slavery happened? Yes! Yet we cannot change history. What we can do is learn from the example set for us by the black slaves....from great difficulty, they created a living beautiful art form.

"Swing Low Sweet Chariot" depicts the faith held by the slaves that someday they would be transported to heaven from this life of toil and trouble. As they worked in the fields, they would sing together. Sometimes the songs had a "call and response" form. A leader would sing a line, such as "Swing low sweet chariot," which was the "call." Then the others would answer singing "Comin' for to carry me home," which was the "response."

One can only imagine the beautiful musical sounds that would rise from the fields where these enslaved people were working. In the elementary classroom, children could act out this musically, with one child being the caller and the rest singing the response. They could draw pictures of the field workers with their hoes and plants growing. The children could experience eating a "hoe cake" which was corn bread made in the field from corn meal and water, patted into a little cake, and baked over an open fire on the metal end of the hoe.

PBS has created a wonderful series and website, *Slavery and the Making of America*. (http://www.pbs.org/wnet/slavery/experience/education/feature.html) This series reminds us that slave songs, usually divided into religious, work, and recreational groupings, provide the origin for jazz, gospel and blues music. What a heritage for us all!

The lyrics of "Follow the Drinking Gourd" told slaves planning to run away how to escape North by night. They were to find the Big Dipper in the sky, represented in the song by the image of a "Drinking Gourd," and move during the dark of night in that direction. Of course, the overseers and land owners were unaware of the double meaning of the beautiful music they were hearing as the slaves were singing in the fields. The use of a gourd for drinking also is descriptive of the life of a slave. In the fields, gourds grew wild, often around fence posts. These gourds could be hollowed out, dried and then used as a dipper to get water. While the slaves were working in the fields, they kept their dippers, which were light weight and had a natural long handle, with them so they could get water from a bucket or creek or pump. Children, by singing the beautiful song together, become part of the history of the Underground Railroad.

Jazz
The music brought by the slaves became mixed with the music sung by African Americans through the centuries and gradually evolved into the truly American art form of Jazz. New Orleans is considered the home of Jazz, and even today one can visit Preservation Jazz Hall and experience the joy of New Orleans Jazz. Jazz has the unique aspect of improvisation, where the performers get up to solo and make up the music as they play. At one point in our history, Jazz was considered inappropriate music to be studied. Now, musicians realize how much musical skill and theoretical understanding is required to be a jazz musician. Jazz influenced European musicians and composers such as Debussy, Milliau, and Stravinsky.

New Orleans is famous for the jazz funeral tradition, in which a group of mourners follows the casket of the dead friend or loved one, forming a sort of parade, singing as they walk along. The music starts slow and mournful, but gradually evolves into joyful exuberant singing. Again, the music of this culture depicts its people's faith. This loved one is not dead, but gone on to heaven, which is a cause for joy!

The Blues
The Blues told in song of the hard times African American people lived in the early 20th century, and continues to be composed and sung today. Hard work, money woes, bad

bosses, love and love lost were all themes sung about in the Blues. The music of the blues is unique because it starts with a sad theme, but through the music is infused a sense of beauty and fun. What a remarkable use of art, to change something bad into something good. Children can write their own blues lyrics, but they must select a topic that gives them "the blues." Homework, tests, something about themselves, such as being slow to get up in the morning might be the topic of the blues. B.B. King is an American Blues icon of our musical culture, who sings the Blues with his guitar he named "Lucille." The teacher could play something from B.B. King, and the children could do reports on his life and music, a very appropriate assignment for Black History Month.

Gospel Music
The Black culture taught us all a lot about living through hard times with grace, beauty, and dignity. Their faith also continued to be told through music. Gospel music to this day is a vital American musical genre. Large Gospel festivals are held throughout America, with different groups presenting gospel music. Usually the music includes a choir, often wearing robes, soloists, choreography with the singers moving as they sing, and an element of improvisation from the solo performers. A Gospel Choir could be created in the elementary school to allow children to experience this type of music.

Holiday Music
Music is part of our celebrations. Christmas carols help us celebrate the Christian holiday of the birth of Jesus. Songs about Santa Claus help us celebrate the tradition of the jolly elf leaving gifts and toys for the boys and girls. This music is appropriate to be sung in the public schools of America if it is taught for musical reasons or for historic/cultural study. Much confusion exists over legal issues surrounding the Separation of Church and State, but the use of music to teach about a culture or used to learn about a specific musical event or device or performance practice is acceptable to use. Music Educators National Conference (MENC) has information concerning the legal use of different types of music considered religious or sacred in nature in our schools. http://www.menc.org/

Christmas in the Big House, Christmas in the Quarters is a children's book that depicts Christmas in the 1880s in Virginia. It shows what the holiday celebration would have been like for the slaves and for the slave owners. One of the traditions described, which started with our Black culture, is the Cakewalk. We think of cakewalks as something done at the elementary school carnival where people walk in a circle to music, and stop on a number when the music stops. Numbers are drawn from a bowl, and the person on the winning number gets the cake. In the African American tradition, couples dance to the music, and the dancers with the most unique, interesting dance moves wins the cake. Usually the older members of the group, those less likely to be among the dancers, were the judges. The French composer Debussy composed a cakewalk, "Golliwog's Cakewalk" for a collection of music, *Children's Suite*, written for his daughter. The Golliwog was one of her stuffed toys. Another children's book, *Mirandy and Brother Wind* is about a cakewalk. The children in an elementary class can do a cakewalk, either the elementary carnival type or the historic type, after reading these books.

Composed Songs to Help Us Teach

"Fifty Nifty United States" is a delightful song, composed by Ray Charles, which lists all the fifty states. Adults who learned that song as children still remember the states by recalling the lyrics.

The music magazine from Plank Road Publishers, *Music K-8*, often has raps or music to help children learn about our country. (Web site is http://www.musick8.com/) The "President's Rap" is a popular item presented by this company.

Music of War

Music can retell our country's history. Each war had music associated with it. The following chart can be the start of research projects to help students learn more about the military history of our country.

War with England for Independence   "Yankee Doodle"

War of 1812   Battle of New Orleans"
                                         A popular song in the 1960s
                                     "Star Spangled Banner"

Civil War   "When Johnny Comes Marching Home Again"
                                     "Dixie"
                                     "The Battle Hymn of the Republic"

World War I   "Caisson Song"

World War II   "Don't Sit Under the Apple Tree with Anyone Else But Me"

Vietnam   "Where Have All the Flowers Gone?"
                                     "If I Had a Hammer"

Hostages in Iran   "Tie a Yellow Ribbon 'Round the Old Oak Tree"
1979

Other Avenues to Learning about Our World

Water, music and the study of civilization

Water has always been important in the study of man. Early settlers searched for land where water was readily available when pushing westward in the expansion of the United

States. Water travel has been important in establishing trade and transportation of goods and people. Music offers compositions about water, which can bring added interest to the historic study of the importance of waterways.

Handel composed Water Music, which was intended to be performed by musicians floating down the Thames River on a barge. This composition would be advantageous to a unit on England, life in the fifteenth century, or to a study of rivers and waterways in Great Britain.

Another programmatic composition about water is Smetana's The Moldau, which tells the story of a ride on a river in Czechoslovakia. (See chapter , pg. For more information.)

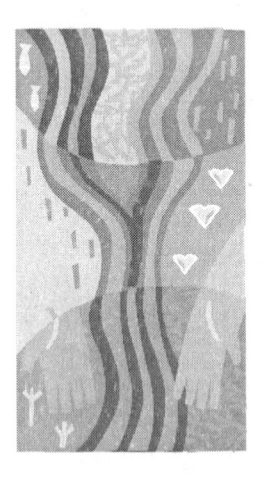

Chapter 10

Relating the Arts

The arts---music, visual art, drama, photography, architecture, poetry, sculpture, dance---contain many similar qualities. Relating them for study is an effective teaching strategy, and helps students compare, contrast and discover ways to use higher level thinking skills.

One of the most commonly used methods to study related arts is through shared historic time periods. As directed by this system or approach, the art of 1850 should be studied with the music of the same time period. As indicated by Dr. Bennett Reimer, noted music educator, this approach to related arts is the least legitimate. Finding arts with similar characteristics for study provides a more valid, authentic learning experience.

> Bennett Reimer (1932 -)   Professor Emeritus from Northwestern University; Author of *The Philosophy of Music Education*, a landmark book in the profession which has been through several editions since the first publication in 1970; authority on curriculum design and aesthetic education.

Art and Music

The Impressionistic period is one historic time frame that allows visual art and music to be justifiably explored together. Both visual art and music from the end of the 19th century through the beginning of the 20th century were moving beyond capturing images and sounds as they had been done previously. After the invention of photography, which made exact imagery possible, artists were less concerned with creating realistic images. They were seeking new ways to visually represent their world.

The artists of the period, including Renoir and Monet, were finding ways to make their art more of an "impression" of the visual. Using colors and light and painting techniques, they created hazy, vague, indistinct images resulting in a whole new type of art.

At the same time, music was moving beyond the traditional sound made by large orchestral pieces, which often used heavy brass instrumentation. The composers were striving for sounds that were new and different. Claude Debussy (1862-1918), a French composer, was exploring a new musical sound. He favored wind and string instruments, with a thin texture. The harp was a favorite instrument of the time. The musical results were an aural correlation to the visual representation of the Impressionist painters.

A quote from Debussy is, "give me music, without sauerkraut, please." Of course, this was an expression of disapproval, a denouncement and rebuke of the music in vogue at the time, often characterized by the music of Wagner, which was heavy sounding, played by large orchestras, and filled with loud brass passages. Wagner, whose operas became the impetus for the Bugs Bunny cartoons where the "diva" Bugs, wearing a helmet with horns and a metal breast covering, sings and torments Yosemite Sam, was also Hitler's favorite composer. Wagner created music that especially fit as the target of Debussy's comment. When you think about it, sauerkraut was a good food analogy.

Music history is filled with a long list of Germanic composers who had gone before Debussy: Bach, Beethoven, Brahms, Schubert, Schumann, all Germanic and all contributors to the historic development of music. Debussy managed to move music beyond this tradition into a sound for which the food comparison would be a soufflé, lemon chiffon cake, or a whipped congealed salad.

One of Debussy's famous orchestral compositions, *Prélude à l'après-midi d'un faune* or *Prelude to the Afternoon of a Faun*, is a good piece for children to hear. Listening to this piece is like looking through a window with a sheer curtain. The children can describe how Debussy achieved this hazy, indistinct feel from the music. (Use of lighter sounding instruments such as the flute, clarinet, violin, harp; having fewer instruments playing at certain points in the music.) Asking the following questions helps them discover the essence of Impressionist music:

- What do you think the fawn is doing? (The often answer "peeking out from the woods," or "softly and quietly walking toward a meadow.")
- What sounds make us have this image of the fawn? (Solo wind instruments, the harp, lots of woodwinds and strings.)
- What is similar between Debussy's music and Impressionistic paintings? (Show a print of Renoir's "Girl with Watering Can" or of one of Monet's Water lilies.)
- Guide the students to see the lighter colors used, the lack of distinct lines, the haziness of the images.
- Both art and music created a feeling of hazy, indistinct imagery. Music through instrumentation and texture and dynamics; art through color and light and brush techniques.

An obvious class activity would be to paint or color an impressionistic art work as the Debussy *Prelude to the Afternoon of a Fawn* is playing in the background. Display the results on a walk collage opposite a display of famous Impressionist art works. Children could do reports on the historic period, on one of the artists or musicians.

Other concepts found among the arts include:

Tension – Release	Smooth – Jagged
Repetition - Contrast	Same -- Different

Architecture and Music

A Picture of Anderson Hall at Kansas State University.
What is the form of this building?
How does the building show the form?
How does music show form?

This building on the K-State campus is an ABA form, demonstrated by the similar wings on either end of the structure, with the taller section in the middle. Also, the windows in the building represent repetition and contrast. Some have an arched top, where others are rectangle. Beside the main door are two windows on either side, each with the arched design. Above those windows are rectangle shaped windows, an excellent example of achieving variety and repetition and balance in design. Music does the same thing. Handel's "Hallelujah Chorus" from *Messiah* is an excellent example of repetition and contrast. It has repetition of themes or motives, which are used to unify the work and achieve balance. The composition achieves variety by changing those melodies and themes. Handel is a master of using repetition and contrast.

Movement and Music
The Red Pony Suite by Aaron Copland includes a section, "Walk to the Bunkhouse" where the rhythms are contrasted very clearly. Children can be grouped and assigned to one of the sections, jagged, smooth or strings.
- Have each group decide on a movement that shows what the music of its section sounds like.
- Play the music, having the groups move demonstrating their selected movement while the music is playing.
- The rule is your group can only move when your music is playing. Strings group moves during "strings sections," Jagged group moves during the "jagged" music sections, and Smooth group moves only during the "smooth" sections of music.

Attending a performance of the *Nutcracker* ballet by Tchaikovsky during the Christmas holiday season is a wonderful opportunity to have elementary age children experience a "real" example of music and movement together. Many ballet companies have performances for school age children, and teachers can write grants to fund the attendance. For schools located in areas far from actual performances, many videos of the *Nutcracker* are available for purchase and can substitute for an actual performance. The children can observe how the dancers' movements illustrate the music. Choreography for the dancers reflects unity, variety and balance (UVB). Dancers achieve UVB through the levels of the movements, which are sometimes low and sometimes high on toes; the location on the stage of the dancers shows UVB, as does their group movement (in a circle or in pairs) contrasted with a more scattered plan with dancers individually moving. Dance is a beautiful art form.

Drama and Music

Acting out the story to "L-Histoire du Soldat" by Stravinsky in Chapter 3, pg. ___ is an good example of relating the arts for teaching purposes. This ballet with narration is a stellar demonstration of relating dance, drama, and music. Operas, such as *The Magic Flute* by Mozart, and ballets, including *The Nutcracker* by Tchaikovsky, demonstrate the relationship among the arts in such productions.

Also, watching a scene from a movie, once without the sound followed immediately by a viewing with sound, is a dramatic demonstration of how much music enhances the dramatic effect of the movie. Watching the opening scene from *Forrest Gump,* where the feather drifts through the air, is a great selection for this activity. The sensation of watching without sound almost makes this scene trite, whereas the addition of the music draws the viewer into the drama.

Unity, Variety and Balance (UVB again)

The arts all make use of UVB strategies to enhance the aesthetic qualities of their medium. Music, visual art, sculpture, photography, dance, architecture, poetry, and drama all utilize repletion and contrast to achieve balance in their art form, and to make it interesting to the viewer, the listener or the audience. Color in visual art can be repeated, where as movements in dance can achieve repetition. Colors of the costumes worn by dancers can be both a unifying and a contrasting technique. Color in music is achieved by the different sounds of the instruments, called tone color. Texture can be used to achieve variety in sculpture or in visual art through the way the stone is cut away or by the brush strokes used to apply the paint. Texture in music refers to the thick or thin sounds of the music achieved through the sounds produced by the various instruments, the number of instruments playing at one time and by the dynamic qualities of the sounds.

Discussing the different art forms can be problematic, as demonstrated by the terms "color" and "texture" in the paragraph above. Part of the reason for this ambiguity or difficulty in using words to describe the arts is inherent in all art because it is often created to provide meaning without the use of words. Some philosophers believe that art gives meaning to life in ways that words can never do. Words are inadequate when describing emotions such as love. Yet, art can capture feelings for us. When one relates a piece of music to an event in life, hearing that music again always transports the person back to that time or event, even if it happened 40 years ago, and it does so in a matter of seconds.

Art is by some believed to be exemplary, an example or illustration, of life. Life has movement, it has hard times and good times, and it is filled with emotional experiences. Art reflects life. Good life has variety, but not so much as to make us feel harried or unsure. Our world has seasons, which provide variety to our lives while at the same time making life unified through predicted repetition year after year. We have night and day, again providing a unifying aspect to life and variety to our days. Art does the same. Life at its best has balance. We don't want to go through final examinations all the time, which would be too stressful. But, we don't want to spend all our time with no stress which would be boring. The arts reflect this. They provide tension and release, again picturing life for us. We certainly don't want to repeat the same day over and over as in the movie *Groundhog Day*. Music that repeated the same tune over and over again would not be interesting to our ears. Composers and performers know how to achieve variety, even within repetition.

Helping students discover the information brought to us through the arts is often a missing part of education. Yet our children, our youth, seek experiences that bring excitement to their lives. The arts can provide a positive outlet for emotional experience. Drugs or DeBussy? Meth or Mozart? I know which I choose for the youth in our schools.

Learning about the arts makes youngsters aware of the differences among us, again reflected through the arts. The arts are unique, each piece of art bringing us different information. Through the study of art, children can begin to realize that different can be good. Because of the differences, particular music or art works become part of our world.

We are not all the same, nor is art all the same. We are tall and short and young and old and all made up with different colors of skin and different appearances. We have blue eyes and brown eyes and hazel eyes and green eyes, and zillions of different combinations of colors and shapes of eyes. We have brown, blond, red, grey and black hair and it can be curly or straight and all sorts of combinations in between. We have big feet and little feet and long arms and shorter arms and all different body types. Our mouths are wide or narrow with lips of different thicknesses, and we speak differently. What a great variety of people we have in this world!

We are ALL DIFFERENT, and that is good. The arts in education teach this well. As a teacher, use and enjoy the study of the arts in your classroom!

Chapter 11   This and That
Lagniappe for the Teacher

Lagniappe is a term used by the Cajun French culture meaning "a little bit more." A bakery in Lafayette, Louisiana, in the heart of Cajun country, might give an extra cookie or two with an order of a dozen. A shop has the practice of giving a little gift, perhaps small hand soaps or a bookmark, just for *lagniappe*.

These ideas are little extras to help you succeed as a teacher. Try them out with your lessons. Make your own list. Keep implementing good teaching practices and watch yourself grow in confidence and skill as a teacher.

Video tape yourself teaching
One of my student teachers dramatically developed his teaching skill during his semester of student teaching. The change was impressive leading me to ask, "How did you do it?" His answer: "I video taped myself teaching everyday. At night, I would watch and find the points in my teaching that I didn't like. I would correct them the next day, and go through the whole process again."

You may not have time to tape everyday, but once a week would be doable. The results will be terrific growth in teaching skill, especially valuable at the beginning of your teaching career. With developments in technology, you could set up the camera on your laptop and tape interactions with students or small groups and evaluate these teaching times as well.

Things to be aware of when you watch yourself on video:

- Eye contact with the students. Are you really paying attention to students when they ask you a question?
- Are you visually sweeping the class periodically during the lesson to make sure students are on task? A common problem of the beginning teacher is unawareness of students off task in the back row, or hitting someone or throwing something while teacher's back is turned!
- Only ask a question when you really want an answer. Don't ask unnecessary questions, such as "Would you like to play the drums today?" This type of question opens the door for students to yell out. If you really want the children to play drums, just state "We are going to play drums today."
- Make sure you give many students opportunities to take part in the learning. One of my student teachers asked a little boy who was usually very disruptive in class to play the bass xylophone. He was thrilled to get the chance, and he told her later that it was the "best day of his life." Giving a child a second chance may change his/her whole attitude about learning.

- Are you walking around as you teach? Don't stand in just one place. Walk among the desks or around the groups of children. It keeps the discipline problems in check and it allows you to see what individual students are doing.
- Make sure you have a visual, an aural and a kinesthetic activity for each lesson. Children learn through seeing, through hearing and through doing. Give each of your students the best chance to learn.
- How are your transitions, when you move from one activity to the next? These are danger spots for the beginning teacher who is inexperienced in keeping students engaged even when moving from one part of the lesson to the next. Questions like, "What was the main thing we learned from reading that paragraph?" can keep students attentive while you are shifting to a new activity.
- Are you speaking loudly enough and projecting your voice so that the children can hear? And conversely, are you varying the level of your voice to keep the children attentively listening?
- Do the children look bored? You may need to add variety to your lesson. Remember that music is a great key to success! Bring in a CD player or boom box and play a variety of music at different times during the day. For art work or seat work, music can lift the atmosphere in the classroom.
- Are you accepting children's comments? Do you make them feel valued by your reaction? Watch that you do not look irritated at some children, even if they do "drive you nuts" by their actions. You are there to help them learn acceptable behavior.
- Do you have a classroom organization, where appropriate responses are spelled out, and where behavior has consequences? Do you consistently apply the rules?
- Are your questions **Making the Children Think**? Questioning so that the answers are beyond yes/no is a mark of an experienced and skilled teacher. One of my former students puts a list of questions on the board before the lesson starts. She writes the questions with a marker on a large piece of brightly colored construction paper and uses a magnet to attach them to the board. The list of questions helps her keep focused on key points of the lesson, and gives the children something to read and look at as she directs their attention to significant information they need to learn.

Welcome to the profession of teaching. We never stop learning and getting better at our practice. Watching yourself teach, although painful at times, is like using *MiracleGrow* on plants. It helps you "grow fast" in your skill level.

Some Favorite Memories from Teaching
My first job was teaching music at Blanton Elementary School in Austin, Texas. The school was named for Annie Webb Blanton, the first female school superintendent in Texas, and also the founder of Delta Kappa Gamma, an education honor sorority. Miss Annie Webb allegedly took office as Superintendent of Schools wearing a large brim picture hat and a flowered dress. As this occurred during the era when teachers wore

black skirts and white blouses with high necks, Annie Webb was making quite a statement about teachers and their wardrobes at her swearing in. From that story about her, I always liked her spunk and was proud to teach at the elementary school named in her honor. An interesting side note about Annie Webb Blanton is that I received the Annie Webb Blanton Scholarship twice from the University of Texas when I later returned to school to pursue my doctorate in music education.

Many precious memories about the students I taught and things they would say and do remain with me. Sometimes they caught me off-guard with their delightful comments, like the day I had them singing songs about the westward movement. We were discussing songs the pioneers might have sung as they moved west in their covered wagons. One little girl raised her hand and asked, "Miss Rudolph, what was it like in the covered wagons?" She thought I had been part of the westward movement, traveling in the wagons myself during the 19th century. My initial thought was, "I'm not that old! How can you think that?" At that time, I was 23 or 24 years old. Now I think, "Wow, I must have done a good job getting her engaged in the lesson. She was really thinking about living on the trail and what it might have been like." Those old songs such as "Oh, Susannah" and "Clementine" are transporters for the children, taking them back to earlier times and enabling them to share history with people who lived over a century before. (Sometimes these days I feel just about old enough to have been part of one of those wagon trains.)

Even when you think you have the students actively involved in the lesson, you may need to take a second look at what you are doing. One time I had my students sitting on carpet squares at the front of the room, all facing the chalkboard. I had written something on the board, a rhythm pattern or musical marking, about the lesson we were learning, and had turned to ask a question about this mark on the board. Every hand was raised! "They all understand!" was my feeling. "Wow, what a great lesson this has been," and "Yippee, I am really getting better at teaching music," were the thoughts swirling around in my head that day. When I called on a child to answer, he said, "Miss Rudolph, You have a runner in your hose." They weren't eagerly wanting to share some deep musical understanding, nor were they poised to answer my question. Instead each child had wanted to tell me about the runner going up the back of my leg. Teaching in the late 60s and early 70s, we were required to arrive each day in a dress with hose; no pants were allowed at all. I got my student's attention alright, just on the wrong thing!

Encouraging participation in my college class
One day we were singing a Canadian children's song, "Alligator Pie" which is sung to a melody loosely based on the American folk song "Shoe Fly." Before we learned the song, I had directed the class to find out the type of pie mentioned in this song.

> Alligator Pie, Alligator Pie,
> If I don't get some I think I'm going to die,
> Take away the green grass, take away the sky,
> But don't take away my alligator pie.

After a rousing version of the song, with many children joining in, as the melody is simple and the words fairly easy to learn, I posed the question again, "What kind of pie is it?" A student, who obviously did not get the gist of my question, which I probably didn't ask as clearly as I think I did, answered "Gooseberry Pie." There were several options I could have taken that day. I could have said point-blank, "No, that is wrong," or I could have talked about the original question which had to deal with the pie mentioned in the song. I could have questioned the student's listening ability. But, I decided to move in a different direction with the class. After saying, "Wow, I love gooseberry pie, especially with a scoop of vanilla ice cream," another student raised her hand and gave the correct answer, "alligator pie."

We agreed that "alligator" was a rather weird type of pie. Then, we sang the song again, this time substituting the words "Gooseberry Pie" but adding new words to the "If I don't get some" part. What could have been a negative experience for one student became a creative opportunity for the whole class. These "going with the flow" experiences in teaching are what give us those excellent "ahaa" moments.

Reinforce the behavior you want to see again
As a beginning teacher trying to get the class focused on the lesson, my tendency was to talk about the ones who were not yet "with me." I would say things like, "Denise, are you having a problem with Seth?" or "Row three, you are not listening." Through a series of training events in our school, I learned a much better way.

In my second year of teaching, we had a visiting team of instructors from the University of Texas conducting research in our school. They were studying the use of positive reinforcement to increase learning. These professors would conduct workshops for our faculty, and discuss methods that encouraged learning positively rather than punitively or negatively. Although I have no idea what became of their research project, the year was a boon to my teaching, and probably redirected my thinking about discipline, classroom management, structuring lessons, questioning skills, and a host of other issues about teaching.

From this year, I learned how to focus on the children who were doing something correctly, rather than on my problems in class. My statements became, "Wow, Susan is ready to begin class. She is sitting tall and listening," and "That group three is really following directions perfectly. I am so lucky to have them in my class." When I learned to use this approach, my discipline problems began to diminish. It sounds simplistic, but it truly worked for me. No longer was I the "drill sergeant" in class, but rather the encourager for learning. At the end of the day, I was much less tired and stressed, and I'm sure my children felt the same.

Of course, I was learning other tricks to teaching as well. One big obvious one was to quickly get into the music of the lesson because music is fun for children. I learned to let the music help me with classroom management. Get the children engaged in the lesson, and they don't give the teacher as many problems.

Eye-contact with the children cannot be overstated. It makes them more accountable for both learning and behavior. Training yourself to be observant of the students is another enormous key to teaching success.

Speaking of keys

Keys come in such an extensive variety of shapes, sizes and functions today. In the time of knights and castles surrounded by moats, keys were heavy and large and made of hand-forged iron. Some keys are very small, like the ones used to open a small chest or jewelry box. Some, like the plastic ones used to open a hotel room, don't even look like keys anymore. The object of a key, however, is still to open something or to start something.

With most aspects of life, we learn what works for us by trial and error. Learning to walk doesn't mean a baby just stands up and walks perfectly right away. It involves a little one going through a lot of falling and getting up again, and going through the process over and over before walking is perfected. Learning is a process, and the process includes failure before success is finally achieved. Learning to teach is no different.

We try something in the classroom, and if it works, we use it again. If it doesn't bring the desired result, we modify or totally change the method. We try another "key." This trial and error approach is useful with teaching. Try a teaching strategy that you have observed or thought of yourself. If it doesn't work, analyze where the malfunction occurred. Design an alternate strategy for that part of the teaching plan. Try it again. You can always bring the children into this trial and error phase. When I was teaching, some of my best ideas started with suggestions from the class.

The door to my music room at Blanton Elementary School had one window at the top. When I was in one of my "trial and error" phases, I would take construction paper and cover up the window, so no one could walk by and see what I was doing. Once I had perfected my approach to teaching a particular lesson, I would uncover the window because I didn't care who observed at that point.

Your path to teaching success may be different from mine or your friend's or your administrator's. Beginning teachers have to find the *keys* that work for them. Although this can be rather frustrating, it is also the reason teaching can be such a rewarding profession. It is never stagnant or dull, new things to learn are always around us as teachers, and each class is different. Teachers constantly have to try out new and different ways to reach their students. Authentic teaching is pulsing with life, always growing and changing, and full of learning for the students and for the teacher.

On an A&E Biography of Laura Bush's life, she said "Teaching is a noble profession," and she is right! Mrs. Bush was a teacher and then a librarian, and one of her desires is to encourage others to become teachers because it is noble work.

A teacher's life is spent helping others learn to succeed. Even as you are trying out new keys, searching for teaching successes yourself, your goal is to help your students learn more effectively. A teacher's desire is for the students to gain knowledge, information, skills, dispositions, behaviors and facts that enable these individuals to become productive members of society. We want our students to be those thriving people. Yes, teaching is a noble profession.

As the preface to this book stated:
> "Some things don't change much Children today still love to play and sing and make music."

Astute teachers will use the natural childhood love of music to their advantage, and let it help them teach. Best wishes to the readers of *Face the Music* as they become part of the noble profession.

Glossary

a cappella --- unaccompanied music. Italian term meaning " in chapel style."

Accent --- A beat that is accentuated, stressed, made louder or accented.

Alto --- The lower female voice category. The second part in 4-part harmony.

Barline--- A line drawn before the accented beat to group the steady beats into sets. It measures the music.

Bass --- The lower male voice category. The fourth part in 4-part harmony.

Coda --- An ending. Literally, it means "tail" in Italian.

Composer --- One who composes music.

Composition --- A composed piece of music.

Compositional Formula --- A system created by Dr. Fallin that helps children create music.

Crescendo --- A dynamic marking meaning gradually getting louder.

Decrescendo --- A dynamic marking meaning gradually getting softer.

Dotted Note --- A dot follows a note, as in dotted half note. The dot indicates half of the value of the note.
    A dotted half note would be held for 3 beats (2 for the half note = 1 for the dot). A dotted quarter note would be held for 1 ½ beats (1 for the quarter note and ½ for the dot).

Double Bar --- A symbol at the end of music.

Double Bass --- The large stand-up stringed instrument, often played in jazz quartets.

Double dotted bar --- A repeat sign.

Dynamics --- One of the musical elements, representing the softs and louds in music. In music, p means soft and f means loud.

Eighth Note --- A type of musical note receiving half a beat in most children's music. Two eighth notes equal one quarter note. ⊓ is the short hand notation for two eighth notes which we call "tee-tee" in class. Division of the beat.

Form --- One of the musical elements. A specific structure in music such as ABA.

Forte --- An Italian term meaning loud. Used in music as a dynamic level, marked with an f, to indicate loud.

Fugue --- A type of "follow-the-leader" form in music. One voice or section plays a melody or theme in the music then another voice enters and plays the same theme, but at a higher or lower pitch. This pattern is followed by several sections or voices.

Genre --- A collection or grouping of something into a category. Like the genre of American folk music.

Half Note --- a type of musical note receiving two beats in music where the quarter note equals one beat.

Harmony --- Two or more notes sounding together. One of the musical elements. Accompaniments such as guitars or piano can create harmony. Voices singing different pitches at the same time create harmony.

Improvisation --- music that is played without writing it out first. It is an section of original performed music, created during a solo part of a jazz composition. The performer must know much about music theory in order to do this type of music.

Introduction ---something that goes before, or at the beginning of a musical composition.

Lyrics --- The words to a song or musical composition.

Measures --- Grouped sets of beats created by the bar lines are called measures.

Melody --- One of the elements of music. The tune of the music.

Meter --- Grouping of beats in duple (2 beats), triple (3 beats) or quadruple (4 beats) meters; created by an accented first beat

Meter Signature--- Numbers appearing at the beginning of music. Top number indicates the number of beats in a measure, and the bottom number indicates the type of note that gets one beat. Sometimes called time signature.

Opera --- A story told in singing. Includes soloists, costumes, orchestra, and sometimes chorus. A dramatic presentation where the story in song is acted out.

Oratorio --- A musical setting of a text, usually sacred. Like an opera in that soloists, orchestra and chorus are included, but it isn't acted out.

Ostinato --- an underlying repeating accompaniment. A boogie-woogie bass is a type of ostinato.
        Plural is Ostinati.

Piano --- An Italian term meaning soft or quiet, and used in music as a dynamic level indicated by p. A keyboard instrument with strings and hammers that hit the strings, causing the sound.

Pitch --- Indicating the up and down movement of melody. Sometimes listed as an element, sometimes replaces "melody" as an element, especially with modern music which has no real melody, but does have "pitches" that move higher and lower.

Programmatic --- A type of music that tells a story in sound, using no words.

Quarter Note --- A type of musical note receiving one beat in most children's music. It is one fourth of the whole note, thus the name "quarter." For the short hand notation in class we use the single line (|)and call it "tah."

Rhythm --- An element of music, including the pulse or steady beat, rhythm patterns, rhythm of the words of the song, division of the beat, note values.

Rhythm Patterns --- Combinations of different rhythms, sometimes can be found in the rhythm of the words. | ⊓ ⊓ |
is a type of rhythm pattern.

Rhythmic Composition --- A composed piece of music made up of rhythm patterns which are performed on instruments or with sounds.

Rondo --- A type of ABACA form. The returning "A" section occurs three or four times.

Soprano --- The highest female voice classification. The first voice in 4-part harmony.

Sound Composition --- Sounds, either made by the children or played by instruments, replace the words of a story or book. The book can be told only in sounds as the pictures are shown.

Steady Beat --- The pulse or "heartbeat" of music. Part of element rhythm, and is what makes us want to tap our toes to the music.

Symphony --- A large orchestra, or a composition for a large orchestra.

Tenor --- The higher male voice category. The third part in 4-part harmony.

Tone Color --- One of the musical elements meaning the sound source, or what is making the sounds in the music. Also called timbre.

Whole Note --- A type of musical note receiving four beats in most children's music.